THE HUNTER'S HAUNCH

Also by Paula Young Lee:

Deer Hunting in Paris: A Memoir of God, Guns, and Game Meat
Game: A Global History
Gorgeous Beasts: Animal Bodies in Historical Perspective
Meat, Modernity, and the Rise of the Slaughterhouse

THE HUNTER'S HAUNCH

What You Don't Know About Deer and Venison
That Will Change the Way You Cook

Paula Young Lee

Skyhorse Publishing

Skyhorse Publishing books may be purchased in bulk at special discounts
for sales promotion, corporate gifts, fund-raising, or educational purposes.
Special editions can also be created to specifications. For details, contact
the Special Sales Department, Skyhorse Publishing, 307 West 36th Street,
11th Floor, New York, NY 10018 or info@skyhorsepublishing.com.

Skyhorse® and Skyhorse Publishing® are registered trademarks of
Skyhorse Publishing, Inc.®, a Delaware corporation.

Visit our website at www.skyhorsepublishing.com.

10 9 8 7 6 5 4 3 2 1

Library of Congress Cataloging-in-Publication Data is available on file.

Cover design by Rain Saukas

Print ISBN: 978-1-62914-661-4
Ebook ISBN: 978-1-62914-999-8

Printed in the United States of America

TABLE OF CONTENTS

PREFACE

Is venison safe to eat? Why does it taste gamy? What can be done to make venison better? For as long as humans have been eating venison, which is a very long time indeed, these questions have been asked and answered in a bewildering number of ways. There are a few reasons why the answers are so inconsistent, but it starts with the fact that people haven't always been talking about the same thing.

Prior to the Industrial Age, "venison" referred to the meat of any traditional game animals taken by hunting. In Europe and England, traditional game animals were chiefly members of the Cervidae family—a group that still includes deer but also elk, caribou, moose, and reindeer—as well as bears and wild pigs. The term "venison" existed in opposition to "cattle," which referred to livestock mammals in general, like cows, sheep, goats, and pigs. In other words, venison did not necessarily come from a deer, moose, or any other cervid.

To be venison, it had to meet two criteria. 1) It had to come from a traditional game animal living in the wild, and 2) it had to have been taken by hunting and not by snaring, trapping, or some other means.

Today's consumers prefer not to think about the animal's life or the means of its taking. Instead, the animal has one name, and its meat has another. So, cows become beef, calves become veal, pigs become pork, sheep become mutton, and deer become venison. It makes no sense to say that pork comes from a cow. Or that mutton comes from a pig. There is a logic to the pattern, and that logic affirms: *if* X animal, *then* Y meat. If deer, then venison. The deer no longer has to be wild, and it does not have to be hunted, for its meat to be called venison.

There are two kinds of (deer) venison: venison that is wild, and venison that is farmed. The farmed kind, which is sold in stores, is becoming more widely available to middle class consumers. The wild version is now generally lower in culinary status because it's perceived to be gamy and possibly "unsafe." This perception is nearly unique to the United States; everywhere else, wild venison is coveted as a culinary delicacy. In part, this is because the United States is the only country where hunting wasn't historically restricted to the nobility or the landed gentry. During the Depression, game meat became sustenance for the impoverished, and anecdotal stories still abound of deer being poached to feed the family. Eight decades later, it is still largely coded as meat for the poor, even as it has been gaining popularity among middle-class locavores and slow food advocates as an organic, nutrient-rich, additive-free meat. For a small group at the very highest end of the economic spectrum, the opportunity to sample true game meat is a sought-after gastronomic experience.

It is certainly true that venison can be gamy to the point of inedibility. It can also be delicious, but it's precisely this unpredictability that distinguishes wild from farmed venison. Wild deer are highly varied in size and habitat, and each species requires different approaches in the kitchen. In the United States, the kinds of deer that can be legally hunted include the robust American whitetail, the blacktail, and the mule deer. In the United Kingdom, "deer" can refer to the small roe deer, the majestic red deer, the fallow deer, the Sika deer, the Chinese Water deer, and the Muntjac—a miniature deer that regularly appears on lists of the World's Strangest Animals because it has fangs and barks like a dog. The red deer is the largest and most prestigious quarry, with the fallow deer a close second.

There are more kinds of deer than these nine, but they are among the most common species and subspecies that can be legally hunted in Europe, the United Kingdom, and the United States. To be successful, game cooks must start by identifying the precise deer they're handling. For example, the pale and delicate venison of the roe deer requires swift cooking and light sauces compared to the red deer. To handle roe deer as if it is red deer will result in dry and rubbery venison. However, the red deer is the more traditional quarry in Europe and the United Kingdom, making it what the old world culinary imagination casts as "real" venison. Much in the same way, in the United States, "real" venison defaults to whitetail. Thus, when Walt Disney made the animated American film *Bambi*, 1942, the title character was a whitetail deer. However, in the original European novel *Bambi*, 1923, the title character was a red deer. Disney made the change in order to avoid confusing American viewers, because there are no red deer in the United States. To American eyes, the red deer looked like a mutant. It was literally an alien species.

At the time, knowing the difference between a whitetail and a red deer was common knowledge, as there were many more hunters and cooks that would have prepared venison regularly. But matters changed quickly. Following the end of the Second World War, an extended period of prosperity meant that consumers no longer needed to know how to

After Thomas Bewick, A hind and a stag of the family of Red-Deer and a Fallow-deer. Wood-engraving, 18th century. Credit: Wellcome Institute.

grow, fish, and hunt for food, let alone how to cook game meat so it tasted good. Seven decades later, only 6 percent of the American population still hunts, meaning that 94 percent of the general public has forgotten how to discern differences among deer species, which mush together into one big-eyed, black-nosed, long-legged symptom of nature's bounty.

Bambi's metamorphosis from red deer into white deer is just one example of a largely unnoticed cultural shift changing how we view wildlife. In this case, a new generation of diners is amazed by the fact that European aristocrats and American settlers used to choke down venison every night for supper. Was venison better in the good old days? Or have palates changed?

✕ CONSIDER THE WHITETAIL

Because it's geographically widespread across the North American continent and also easy to identify, the whitetail has become the iconic symbol of American wildlife. Like all members of the Cervidae family, the whitetail deer (*Odocoileus virginianus*) is a hooved herbivore. A male whitetail is a buck. A female is a doe. A juvenile is a fawn. Though it can graze (head down), it prefers to browse for food (head up), favoring berries, leafy bushes, and tree buds. Large bodied with slim legs, the adult whitetail ranges in size from 90-pound does to 300-pound bucks. Its pelt is brown with a white belly, and its most distinctive characteristic is the white underside of its tail, which it raises like a warning flag to alert other members of the herd. Fawns are reddish-brown and spotted. Mature bucks have pronged antlers, which they drop every year following the mating season, called the rut.

Whitetail doe. Credit: Michael Witzel (Wikimedia Commons).

In the United States, the whitetail is so ubiquitous that books about deer hunting typically lay out the best strategies for hunting this particular species. The whitetail is the ongoing focus of the large and well-organized Quality Deer Management Association, which provides an annual report on the state of the species. Over the past few decades, wildlife biologists have closely studied the biology, habitat, mating patterns, population numbers, diseases, and behaviors of the whitetail deer. This information grows daily, because deer hunting generates large revenues for the tourist industry, along with commercial sales of outdoor gear and sporting equipment. The 2012 National Survey of Fishing, Hunting, and Wildlife-Associated Recreation (FHWAR), issued by the United States Department of Fish and Wildlife Service, estimated that 13.7 million people (6 percent of the adult population in the United States) went hunting in 2011. Of this group of hunters, 11.6 million individuals (85 percent) pursued large game such as elk and deer. An additional 33 million people went fishing.

Six percent doesn't sound like a lot, but the United States is a big country. By any other measure, 11.6 million hunters is a large number of enthusiasts, especially given that they are mostly interested in a single species: whitetail deer. Currently, there are over 4 million whitetail in Texas alone, and an estimated 30 million in the country. A legal hunter gets one tag per deer, but of course getting a tag is not a guarantee of a kill: 11.6 million hunters does not automatically translate into 11.6 million deer heads mounted on walls. Far from it. Ironically, hunting has less of an impact on the deer populations than the high rate of vehicular collisions, which is now responsible for the majority of deer fatalities in this country. Hunters would like it very much if American drivers would stop running into deer, as it makes the challenging task of hunting even more difficult.

Until you go looking for them, whitetail seem to be everywhere. Then they're invisible. Even in today's fame obsessed world, wild deer don't stand around posing for the paparazzi. They look like a furry blur, a flap of a warning tail, or a wet and curious nose.

Because deer spend a lot of time making sure you can't see them, researchers have constantly updated best hunting practices with the latest scientific information. The same updating, however, has not held true regarding the treatment

Whitetail in my front yard in Maine, 2014. Credit: author.

of the venison. Instead, venison has long been framed as an afterthought or by-product of the hunt, and either consumed out of obligation or discarded because it's in such bad shape that it's not worth the effort to salvage.

To remedy this situation, *The Hunter's Haunch* investigates the impact of history, hunting traditions, cooking habits, and folklore on the preparation of wild venison, thereby positioning venison as a component of the hunt itself. Because culinary interest in wild game is relatively recent, serious attention has not yet been paid to the impact of hunting practices on the quality of the venison. Instead, one of the few stabs at synthesizing the killing, cooking, and consumption of a wild animal is a famous essay by novelist David Foster Wallace. "Consider the Lobster," 2005, is a strange essay made even more strange for the fact that *Gourmet* published it. Wallace's struggles to grapple with the idea of preparing lobster, which is just about the only wild animal that American housewives will admit to killing with their own two

hands, demonstrate just how little today's consumers under-
stand regarding the relationship of animal life to the food on
their plates. Wallace observed:

> A detail so obvious that most recipes don't even bother
> to mention it is that each lobster is supposed to be alive
> when you put it in the kettle. This is part of lobster's
> modern appeal: It's the freshest food there is. There's
> no decomposition between harvesting and eating.

He's correct; lobster recipes tend to leave this information out. If you ask the fishmonger, he will tell you what to
do with them, but he will think you're either an idiot or a for-
eigner for not already knowing how to cook them. Albeit in a
very odd way, Wallace also points out that cooks who try to
dispatch the lobster more "humanely" by microwaving, stabbing, or slowly raising the temperature of the lobster instead
of dropping it in boiling water, are not only performing con-
ceptual somersaults around the lobster's basic anatomy, but
deluding themselves regarding the human capacity for moral
relevancy. It's also the case that Wallace didn't catch the lobster. He mostly stared at it. Perhaps if he had put in the weeks
of work to obtain the lobster himself, he might have felt dif-
ferently about things. In the end, despite his ethical qualms,
Wallace ate the lobster anyway. But, like Henry David Thoreau before him, he felt elaborately, exhaustively bad about it.
As with the lobster, part of venison's "modern appeal"
is that it's fresh, wild, and replete with nostalgic value. It's
got a certain culinary cachet, tastes better with butter, and
the wild version is becoming increasingly inaccessible at
all social levels. As that inaccessibility increases, so do the
myths informing its preparation. Lobsters turn red when
boiled, and venison dries out when roasted. This "obvious"
information gets left out of recipes, leaving gaps that only
become problems when common knowledge isn't so common
anymore. The older the recipe, the larger the blank spaces.

With each successive generation, the reasons behind certain conventions have become obscured or totally lost. One of the goals of *The Hunter's Haunch* is to reexamine those inherited practices. Why did they work 100 years ago? Do they still work today? Knowing what we do today, how can we adapt that passed down knowledge to our culinary advantage?

To recap:
- "Venison" used to include the meat of any game animal taken by hunting.
- "Venison" now chiefly refers to meat from deer, including farmed deer.
- In the American context, "deer" means whitetail.
- In the British and European context, "deer" means red deer.

Even within the same species, however, the taste, toughness, and texture of venison can vary so widely that many cooks wonder how it's possible that it never seems to behave the same way twice. It's because the flavor, tenderness, and palatability of wild venison depends on 1) the deer's diet, 2) the time of year it was taken, 3) the geographical region where it was living, 4) the age of the animal, 5) the sex of the animal, 6) its overall health, 7) if female, whether it was pregnant, 8) whether it was hunted well or badly, 9) if it was correctly field dressed, and finally, 10) if it was hung, and for how long. The first seven variables depend on the wildness of a wild animal. The last three reflect the care and skill of the hunter.

None of these factors involve cooking. Even when the hunter is the cook, it is only after the carcass enters the kitchen that culinary skills impact the quality of the dish. In other words, wild meat is the record of a good hunt, along with everything that entails. Delicious venison starts all the way back with the decision to hunt in order to put food on the table—a decision that changes strategy, timing, setup, even weapon and ammo. If your venison is inedible, consider these common errors:

1. ... *Aiming with the ego.* The best eating is not the aggressive trophy buck with the biggest rack. The best eating is calm and young, which means a pronghorn buck or a doe.
2. ... *Making a bad shot.* If you bungle your shot and the deer starts to run, it spells disaster for your supper.
3. ... *Poor field dressing.* Bring field dressing tools and a tarp, and know how to proceed before starting a hunt.
4. ... *Careless butchering.* Bucks have scent glands. They smell bad and taste worse. Don't let it get on the meat or your hands.
5. ... *Ignoring biology.* A carcass wants to be cooled as fast as it can. Neglect this step at your digestive peril.
6. ... *Not planning for bad weather.* Too warm/too cold for hanging damages the venison. Shift the carcass to a meat locker.
7. ... *Leaving the cuts untrimmed.* Fat goes rancid. Trimming knives are your friend.
   And, finally:
8. ... *Confusing venison with beef.* How it looks raw isn't how it cooks up. Know the cut.

Again, out of these eight errors, only the last one has anything to do with cooking techniques. Surprisingly, the recipe itself is the least important factor in determining the deliciousness of the dish. If the venison starts out in good shape, the cook's main job is to make sure not to ruin it. Terrific venison only needs a hot pan, a bit of oil, sea salt and cracked pepper to be exceptional in taste and texture. But if the deer is badly hunted, it won't matter if the chef smothers it in sautéed truffles with a side of honey-glazed squash flowers. It will be terrible. *The Hunter's Haunch* hopes to help hunters avoid this tragedy by explaining why and how it happens in the first place.

INTRODUCTION

× **HUNTING FOR FOOD**

Cooking with wild ingredients means always working with some degree of uncertainty. Some seasons, there's abundance. Others, there's scarcity. In the mid-20th century, American deer populations were low. Now, thanks to sustained conservation efforts, these populations are extremely high. They are, in fact, so high that deer are becoming environmental nightmares, damaging forests and rupturing ecosystems. Thus, organizations such as The Nature Conservancy permit deer hunting on its lands, arguing that it cannot allow a single species "to become so out of balance with its historic natural numbers that many plants found on our lands, including rare or endangered ones, are threatened with their very existence." Hunting is the traditional method to restore balance, which includes consuming venison out of respect for the deer's wild existence.

Whitetail deer are now in the city, in the country, in the streets, and in the suburbs. In some parts of the country, chiefly in the Northeast corridor, deer are so plentiful they're viewed as furry locusts. Tame, they feast on forsythia and decorative trees, and they don't run away from cars (they *do* flee pet dogs, which in their minds likely trigger the same response the same as wolves, the dog's wild ancestor). Suburban deer are soft and plump. They are basically "free-ranging" semi-domesticated deer, halfway between wild and farmed.

It may seem like it's easy to throw a rock at one and drag it back into the kitchen. But, like many things in modern life, it's not so simple. In the United States, hunting is open to everyone, but 1) you have to have a hunting license, and 2) there are laws, which vary per state. Per season, a hunter gets one tag per wild animal. Across the spectrum of wildlife, the tagging system is consistent, with the number of tags allotted varying by species and by state, reflecting the populations of indigenous wildlife. There are no gator tags distributed in Maine, for example, because Maine has no native wild alligators. Allotments also vary from year to year depending on the health of the herd/flock and other statistics. In areas of the country where deer populations are heavy, such as New Jersey, hunters might be allotted several tags. In other states where deer populations are low, such as Vermont, hunters might only get one tag per season. Or no tags at all.

A tag sets the legal limit per hunter that season. Applying for and receiving a deer tag (which comes with a fee) is no guarantee that the hunter will even see a buck that year. Some seasons, even experienced deer hunters may wind up with no venison in their freezer. But regardless of whether a hunter in the United States has filled one tag or ten, that venison can be consumed at home or given to friends but may not be sold.

By contrast, in the United States and most of the world, it *is* legal to sell venison from deer raised on deer farms. Though farmed deer are raised under human management, they are frequently and confusingly called "wild venison" on upscale menus and packaging labels. In this country, there is an easy way to tell if your venison comes from a semi-domesticated deer that grew up with fences: if cash money bought it and there was a receipt, the venison came from a deer farm. This is also true of packaged venison carried by large chain stores in the United Kingdom such as Waitrose or Sainbury's, where shoppers expect to find venison next to beef, chicken, and pork in the Meat section.

In order to make farmed venison more consumer friendly, the deer farm industry is striving to establish a rating system that helps ensure consistency. This kind of product conformity is very helpful to chefs, because it means they will know what to expect. Industry standards means that a venison steak purchased this week will be the same in taste, texture, and consistency as a venison steak purchased next week, next month, and next year. Standardization ensures predictability.

What this boils down to is that the difference between wild vs. farmed venison is ultimately about a relationship. The first, "wild," is a relationship between the hunter and the quarry. The second, "farmed," is a relationship between the consumer and the meat. The hunter-quarry relationship conserves the possibility that the human may go hungry. The consumer-meat relationship takes that worry away and provides a money-back guarantee. This security not only turns the deer into a cow, it transforms the human into a shopper: a vehicle for making money move around quickly.

We are all consumers now. But some consumers are also hunters. They would rather be consuming venison and not beef. And they would like that venison to be as delicious as possible. Why, then, do so many hunters end up with venison that's inedible?

× THE FAT OF THE LAND

Over the course of the 20th century, one of the most profound dietary shifts in the United States has been the rejection of wild ingredients in favor of a near-total dependency on factory-farmed foods. "In fact gaminess is becoming rare," notes Mark Bittman, the author of *How to Cook Everything*, 2008, who adds: "starkly gamy flavors are hard to take for people who were not raised on them." Venison's rich concentration of flavors—which is not the same as being "gamy"—can shock contemporary palates habituated to sweet, bland food. In other words, it's possible that your hunted venison isn't bad. It just tastes too strong, in the same way that black coffee is too bitter for those who take it with cream and two sugars.

According to Elizabeth II's personal chef, she dines on venison every night, suggesting that it's not just consumed when there's no better options around. Because game remains popular in Britain, where venison is still coded to economic and political power, it's worth bringing forward the fact that it used to be routinely served at the 19th-century White House. One sample buffet menu for 1,000 guests included Cold Game in Season, Game Pig, and Venison with Currant Jelly. Helpfully, the *White House Cookbook*, 1887, provided extensive instructions regarding the correct method of presenting, slicing, and serving this haunch, including detailed diagrams.

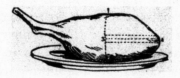

The haunch in question comes from a deer that must have been morbidly obese, but all the more desirable for that reason. A century ago, cooks knew that a superior haunch of venison began with the wild berries the doe had been feasting on all summer, for it infused the flesh with sweet, fruity notes, turning venison into the meat version of a fine wine and its tasting into a culinary ritual. The *White House Cookbook* listed a few variables that affected the cooking process: doe venison cooks up faster than buck venison; the finest meat comes from a young stag, followed by a doe; it's best to take deer in autumn because that's when they're most fat.

Here's the trouble: I've never run into a deer so overweight that it waddled through the woods. If anything, the opposite tends to be true: deer are flighty creatures that spend their lives running away from everything. All that running means that they tend to be exceptionally lean: there's very little subcutaneous fat, and certainly no marbling. "Marbling" refers to intramuscular fat or fat that runs throughout the muscle fibers, giving it a marbled appearance. Cuts that have the most marbling are the most desirable, as fat imparts flavor. By starting out fattier, a marbled cut tends to maintain tenderness while cooking; it's the fact that it doesn't dry out as easily that prompts cooks to associate marbling with tenderness. Crucially, marbling is genetic, not a function of overeating, and can vary greatly among breeds. Hence Wagyu cows, which make Kobe beef, are prized for the exceptionally concentrated marbling of their meat and the nutritional value of their fat. By contrast, lifelong overeating resulting in obesity produces layers of fat beneath the skin (subcutaneous or "fluffy" fat) and around the organs (hard fat or suet).

The bottom line is that fat isn't just "fat." It's a metabolic substance vital to good nutrition. Without it, we cannot assimilate certain vitamins, so it's added to a lot of packaged foods but largely missing from game. With the exception of wild mammals that hibernate, such as bears, dormice, and groundhogs, or those that live in exceptionally cold climates, such as polar bears and seals, a lack of subcutaneous fat characterizes wild animals in general. Wild pigs are dry compared to their domesticated counterparts, and wild rabbits are so lean that humans forced to survive on them will die of a form of malnutrition called "rabbit starvation," the food equivalent of dying of thirst while gulping down gallons of salt water. Rabbit starvation had plagued early American colonists, who eventually figured out that they'd suffer badly and even die from malnutrition without a reliable source of animal fat to supplement their diet. Centuries later, scientists discovered the cause of this seeming paradox of eating so much game meat that you starve to death: it's because rabbits, hares, and other members of the *Leporidae* family are nearly pure protein.

Too much protein will overload the capacity of human kidneys and liver to process urea and amino acids. Sufferers quickly begin to display the dismal symptoms of food deprivation: distended belly, diarrhea, constant hunger, and fatigue. Yet the immediate solution to rabbit starvation is also very simple: in *Never Cry Wolf,* wildlife biologist Farley Mowat noted that his decision to survive in the wild by exclusively eating wild meat—in his case, field mice—made him feel progressively worse until he figured out he had to eat the entire mouse, including guts, skin, and eyeballs, thereby obtaining essential fatty acids and other nutrients absent from the muscle itself but abundantly present in fat.

If Mowat had consulted cookbooks written before 1900, he might have saved himself some trips to the latrine. Cookbooks used to routinely recommend cracking bones for marrow and tenderly slicing up the brains. Classic recipes for hare nearly always included the kidneys, the heart, and the liver, all chopped up and served in a delightful blood sauce. Under ordinary circumstances, these innards are so tiny that it hardly seems worth the bother to sauté them. The culinary tradition can seem baffling, but we now know that it reflected practical considerations that went far beyond Yankee frugality. The pinnacle of haute cuisine is still *ris de veau* (calf sweetbreads: thymus, pancreas, and lymph nodes) and *foie gras*, goose liver, for these organs enjoy high concentrations of fat. It now seems obvious that these rich sauces weren't just for flavor. These recipes reflect years of collective experience regarding the particular quirks of cooking wild game, binding good taste to a healthy desire to not die, as a survivalist might say… or to live well, which is exactly the same idea expressed by a more optimistic personality.

From a culinary perspective, the value of fat cannot be overstated. Thus, on the one hand, it makes sense that the *White House Cookbook* recommended that venison be served on warm plates and the haunch kept in chafing dishes in order to keep its fat loose and translucent. (This advice is sound: as soon as venison starts to cool, it dries out and stiffens far more quickly than other red meats.) On the other hand, it's mystifying that the White House's head chef found himself facing a haunch of venison so fatty that it was "like mutton." The rind of a domestic sheep's hind leg can be several thumbs thick with fat. For this reason, a leg of lamb is lovely when roasted. Yet hunter after hunter will attest that venison from a whitetail deer has hardly any fat at all.

Rabbit starvation isn't limited to rabbits, but extends to any diet that relies too exclusively on game as a staple. Unhelpfully, it is also the case that 20th-century game cookbooks invariably instruct cooks to start by ruthlessly trimming their venison, insisting that even the tiniest hint of external fat will impart an offensive flavor to the dish. So which is it? Is venison fat tasty, or terrible? Is there a lot of it, or hardly any? Perhaps, a hundred and fifty years ago, herds of deer were living off the cornucopia of the land and becoming roly-poly as a result. Have the tables since turned, and now we're the ones waddling through the woods, searching for a skinny deer for supper?

So I puzzled. I researched. I cooked. And as I learned more about hunting and cooking wild animals, the answer became clear: the haunch of venison served at the White House was not from a wild deer. It almost certainly came from a semi-domesticated deer raised in a deer park. Up through the Industrial Revolution, wealthy nobles in Europe, the United Kingdom, and Asia kept private deer parks to supply their dinner tables. That arrangement appealed to parvenu Americans, who emulated it. The outlines of deer parks can still be found in older residential communities in the United States, chiefly in New England, though they've fallen completely out of use for the purposes of keeping managed herds of deer. Its most recent permutation is the commercial deer farm, which is a similar operation with one major difference: it is not private, but tied to the demands of the marketplace. Globally speaking, the largest deer farms are located in New Zealand, which is also known for its sheep industry.

Deer farms shield semi-domesticated deer from predators and often feed them with grain. The deer no longer need to forage for browse, or fear getting run over by cars. They can become quite plump, and their fat is mild and sweet because the sedentary lifestyle directly affects the flavor. Perhaps most importantly, however, these conditions guarantee a tasty haunch of venison by the end of the day. This predictability is desirable when serving a thousand important guests who are seated at a formal table and reading elegant menus printed with the words: "Venison with Current Jelly." But for many hunters, this guarantee means that this meat isn't venison. Philosophically speaking, it's beef. The animal may be a deer, but the human management of its daily routine has turned it into a cow.

From the hunter's perspective, farm-raised deer and wild deer might as well be unrelated species. Same goes in the kitchen, meaning that cooks must begin by knowing which kind of venison they're trimming. Why is farmed venison so different from wild venison? Among other things, farmed meat comes with a label. Wild meat doesn't. In the grocery store, cooks begin by deciding the protein they wish to serve for supper—that is, meat, fish, poultry, or soybeans—and then determine which cut (filet mignon, fish sticks, chicken breast, extra-firm tofu, etc.) they can afford. It's not the genus but the price per pound that shapes cooking decisions. The antithesis of farmed meat, wild venison presents a challenge because consumers aren't used to thinking about the biography of their food.

When meat is farmed, pre-slaughtered, pre-butchered, and sold pre-wrapped, it is cut off from its personal history as an individual animal, as well as its inherited legacy as a member of a group that has lived with humans for centuries. Whether livestock or pet, all domesticated animals (… vegetables, grains, fruits, etc.) have been profoundly manipulated to serve human needs. Consider the chicken (*Gallus gallus domesticus*), a domesticated creature that comes in an astonishing variety of breeds. Humans eat a lot of these birds. According to the Food and Agricultural Organization of the United Nations, in 2009 the world consumed approximately 92.9 million tons of poultry. The chicken is expected to cook up a certain way. It can be fried, grilled, boiled, roasted, sautéed, shredded, breaded, and shaped into fingers and nuggets. What this "versatility" mostly reveals is that the chicken has been bred to be foolproof.

The perfect recipe for roast chicken is by chef Thomas Keller, who requires one "farm-raised" chicken, a bit of butter, and a dash of Dijon mustard if you like. The genius of this recipe resides in the instructions that follow: "Rinse the chicken, then dry it very well with paper towels, inside and out." No basting, no fussing while it roasts serenely for 50 or 60 minutes, then take it out and let it rest for 15 minutes before carving. Dry high heat + internal fat = perfect roast chicken.

The recipe works because certain realities about the chicken are baked into the bird. There are layer hens for eggs, roosters for breeding, and fancy chickens kept as pets, but the kind that gets fried is a broiler chicken bred for millennia to be docile and delicious. The fact that your particular hen might be farm-raised and eating bugs, worms, and seeds as it ranges over grassy fields doesn't fundamentally alter approximately 8,000 years of selective breeding for two specific qualities: to appeal to the human palate, and to reach maturity quickly.

Domesticated chickens are plump with fat. Even the skinny specimens are several orders of magnitude fattier than that wild progenitor of domesticated chickens, the Red Junglefowl (*Gallus gallus*). Some domesticated chickens are so free ranging that they've gone completely feral, but the most complicated chicken recipes in the world won't produce a delicious roast if the chicken started out wild. Try using Keller's recipe on a Red Junglefowl that's been raised on an American farm, technically making it a "farm-raised chicken," and the result will be an inedible football.

Many steps went into shaping the chicken bird before it became chicken meat, and just as many steps affect the deer before it becomes venison. But as long as the animal is wild, its meat will be too. How it lived, and how it died, affects the taste and texture of the venison. A bad hunter makes bad venison no matter how pampered the deer, but a good hunter can end up with terrible venison too, if the winter's been hard that year. For these reasons and more, wild meat is more complex than meat bought at the store, where every inch of the animal's life and death has been under human control. The absence of that control changes everything, including the way the cook must approach the task at hand.

CHAPTER ONE
Going Wild: Getting to Wild Meat

× THE HUNTING QUESTION

In modern society, hunting is the sort of activity that raises hackles as well as eyebrows. Why hunt for food, the urban sophisticate wonders, when there's a grocery store on every corner and restaurants lining the streets? There are lots of ways to respond to that question, but recent books on hunting typically argue that subsistence hunting itself restores a kind of essentialist balance between man and nature. To hunt, the argument goes, allows *homo sapiens* to reenter the world as an engaged being who needs all five senses to connect with nature, which includes chasing it down and celebrating its life by serving it for supper. At the other end of the spectrum, generational hunters will shake their heads at such nonsense, wipe off their hands on their pants, and go straight for the jugular as they chop off Bambi's head. The former tends to quote Ortega y Gasset and Brillat-Savarin, best known for the sobriquet, "Tell me what you eat and I will tell you who you are." The latter drowns all doubts in Hotter n' Hell barbecue sauce, and thinks toilet paper is for sissies.

As far as I'm concerned, neither existential ennui nor high standards of personal hygiene will rescue your venison if you've approached it the wrong way—and that "wrong" way still has to do with belief systems, they're just belief systems regarding the limits of edibility. I'm often asked if venison is safe to consume, as if hand-caught food was inherently germy, full of stealthy bacteria eager to invade weak and foolish immune systems. Those are cultural expectations talking, meaning there's nothing "natural" about those fears. Rather, they're the product of two centuries' worth of cultural narratives pushing wildness out of everyday life as an insult to polite society.

A good example of the success of these narratives is Jo Robinson's *Eating on the Wild Side*, 2013, which has nothing to do with hunting for wild meat or foraging for wild plants. It's a guidebook for picking out the "most nutritious" fruits and vegetables at the grocery store. Robinson is disappointed by the average vegetable's low levels of phytonutrients, which are plant-based chemicals such as ephedrine and lycopene. (Just think "antioxidants." Which are like "electrolytes." In other words, they're naturally occurring chemicals that make certain plants beneficial for humans.) Her book leaves out dairy, fish, poultry, and meat, as none of these animal-based food sources has phytonutrients. They can't. This is because fish, birds, and mammals are not plants. Animals don't have roots or leaves, and their cells do not derive energy via photosynthesis, which is the process leading to the "phyto" (meaning "green") in "phytonutrients." Animal protein *does* have amino acids and B vitamins, but Robinson isn't interested in these things.

Me neither. It's now commonplace to argue for dietary choices using nutritional claims, with "empty calories" being akin to moral bankruptcy, and "high nutritional value" being the best investment of your grocery money. But I'm not per-suaded by the "it's good for you!" argument, because most food is good for you, even the food that is supposedly bad. Having nothing to eat is the real trouble for a good chunk of people on the planet. Sure, venison is an all-natural, low-fat source of high-quality protein, but so are snails and earth-worms. If an optimal ratio of calories to nutritional value was a primary motive for food choices, then beetles and other insects ought to be on Special this week at Whole Foods™. Instead, when half of an inchworm shows up in the last bite of an organic heirloom apple, it's grounds for a lawsuit.

On every level, the relationship of man to meat is more complex than simply deciding that wild is bad and domesticat-ed is good, or vice versa. Real life is messy, and claiming the moral high ground regarding the "rightness" of certain foods ignores the sheer difficulties of eating well in the contempo-rary world. In the desert, there is insufficient water for crops. In the Arctic, the growing season is too short, etc. Where humans can survive, so can other mammals. But crops? Not necessarily. Agricultural control contributes to the health of the marketplace, but is not always to the benefit of humans as a species. The negative effects of the long-term manipulation of cultivars is partly Robinson's point, as we have bred fruits and vegetables for looks instead of flavor, and created fruits so sweet that they now cause diabetes.

Dutifully, now, journalists raise the alarm about lowered levels of phytonutrients and point out the deception of cute farms that are actually mega-corporate-industries, but there's nothing sexy about soil depletion from overplanting, or the fact that the thousands of acres of fields planted with am-ber waves of grain exist at the expense of the wildlife. But because these realities are true, none of us are morally pure in this food business. If you eat, you're swallowing a life and maybe even a soul, and that goes for vegetarians too. That uncomfortable truth got to be such a conundrum for Thoreau that he pretty much decided that no eating of anything whatsoever should be allowed. He associated meat with "uncleanliness," but concluded that abstinence from "food of any kind" was the pathway to transcendence. For those who prefer not to starve to death, it's more practical to acknowledge that humans participate inside a food ecosystem, and to face it without excuses or pretense.

× "HUNTING" VS. "HARVESTING"

In the introduction to *A Hunter's Heart: Honest Essays on Blood Sport*, 1997, David Petersen railed against the "harvesting" of deer and other wild animals. He didn't object to hunting. He objected to the word "harvesting." One of this country's most respected advocates of backcountry hunting, Petersen thought that this "ugly" word exposed the "meanest, cruelest" human attitude to nature, for it reduced the relationship between man and animals to an economic equation.

The equation is bad for the wildlife, because the concept of "harvesting" meat traces its roots back to the wide-scale implementation of the slaughterhouse system. A French and British institution perfected in the United States, the slaughterhouse is the invention of a 19th-century middle class that disdained the smells and sounds of farm animals. Initially, the public objected to the loss of hand-butchered beef, but was gradually won over by the ready availability of inexpensive fresh meat in the name of public hygiene (the "cleanliness" that Thoreau obsessed over). In the United States, the slaughterhouse is also called an abattoir. This word comes from the French word *abattre*, a forestry term that referred to cutting down trees. When the term migrated to the military, it referred to cows being felled to feed hundreds of hungry troops. With the rise of the slaughterhouse, the term became fully aligned with what ethnographer Noelie Vialles called a "vegetalized" vision of livestock. Inside this vision, livestock is not slaughtered but "harvested" in the manner of trees cut down in the woods.

It would be easy to dismiss Petersen's dislike of "harvesting" as prissiness. Fruit is harvested, wheat is harvested, berries are harvested, and now, meat is harvested. Boohoo. Who cares, since all it does is make it harder for tree huggers to justify their antihunting views? But when slaughter is practiced on an industrial scale, the animal becomes reduced to meat-on-the-hoof, not a life but a set of losses and profits inside the stock market. Livestock animals used to hold a variety of roles, providing milk, muscle, and manure. Their life, as well as their death, reflected pragmatic considerations related to the harsh realities of single-family farming. A century later, the animal's central role inside an agricultural economy has vanished from consumer consciousness. The palate now favors the mishmash that is ground beef, a grind for the daily grind. Bits of prime rib, shoulder, brisket, shank, and gristle ... from high to low, expensive to cheap, the scraps of classed cuts are rendered indistinguishable, making ground beef the most politically optimistic of meats and the hamburger the most egalitarian of meals. The cow's age and gender have also vanished from the meat in the supermarket shelves, replaced by labels warning "best if sold by" as the only dates that matter.

To all extents and purposes, livestock animals are now farmed in the same manner as staple crops: grown in mass quantities, harvested by machines, and packaged in a factory. This system, it is claimed, is better than hand-slaughter and makes subsistence hunting obsolete, for consumers never have to face a living animal in order to obtain meat. From the consumer's perspective, there is no blood, no confrontation with death, and no mess to clean. Therefore it is more civilized. As it passes through the system, the cow is stunned, bled, gutted, skinned, hung, cooled, butchered, and shrink-wrapped, but at no step in this sequence does it officially die. The first step, 1) stunning, doesn't kill but renders it unconscious, for 2) when it is bled, blood drains best when the heart is still beating, and 3) gutting is not immediately lethal. Neither is 4) skinning. At some point along the way, the cow certainly dies.

But, according to the logic of the machine, the person who dooms the cow, the pig, and the chicken is the kindly grandpa in overalls who allowed their conception in the first place.

As reporter Christopher Leonard established in *The Meat Racket*, 2014, the slaughterhouse system extends to nearly every farm and grocery store in present-day America, the meat production of which is controlled by just four conglomerates. One of these four, Tyson Foods, slaughters 135,000 head of cattle, 391,000 hogs, and 41 million chickens every week. The numbers are staggering, yet how this happens remains largely invisible and, despite Leonard's work, unthinkable. The critiques are as old as the system itself and have had no effect. Over time, the system has merely strengthened.

Though it would appear that the vegan rather than the hunter is the archenemy of this meat-making machine, veganism is actually a direct extension of the factory farm system. By demanding year-round supplies of fruits and vegetables, consumers have transformed produce into a product. Try growing wheat in the backyard, and see how far that crop goes toward homemade flour for pasta, bread, pancakes, waffles, muffins, cookies, and pie crusts. Or try growing apples in winter. Or tomatoes in the desert. Etc. To be able to eat what you want, when you want it, is a consequence of economic power and social technologies that are the true nature of "natural" food.

In a popular "wartime supplement" cookbook published between the Wars (WWI and WWII) and again during the Great Depression, the Mystery Chef laid it out plainly: "At least ten thousand people help you prepare each meal," he noted, and these people are working-class and thus invisible to those doing the eating. To explain, the Mystery Chef (a Scotsman who moved from London to New York) did what Michael Pollan repeated seventy years later: he traced one ingredient from field to plate. Instead of corn, the Mystery Chef followed wheat.

Carl Hassman, [The meat market], Puck (June 13, 1906). Illustration shows a butcher labeled "The Beef Trust" standing behind a counter in a butcher shop; around him are meat products labeled "Potted Poison, Chemical Corn Beef, Bob Veal Chicken, Tuberculosis Lard, Decayed Roast Beef, Deodorized Ham, Embalmed Sausages, and Putrefied Pork. A verse from the Bible appears below the counter: "Therefore I say unto you, Take no thought for your life, what ye shall eat, or what ye shall drink. Matthew VI: 25."

The farmer has planted the seed and it has grown to maturity—a waving field of golden grain in the Northwest…. First there are the men who sowed and cultivated the grain, and then the threshing machines and the men who run them. Now the trucks are hauling the wheat to a ship in the Great Lakes. Follow that ship—watch the stokers as they shovel coal (and don't forget the miners who mined the coal which drives the ship's engines). The ship carries the grain to a great flour mill with its roaring machinery, and here a vast number of men is employed. Then there are the cotton pickers in the South who pick the cotton that feeds the looms that weave the sacks in which the flour is put. And there are the printers who print the name on the sack in order that you and I may be able to recognize the brand of flour that we want—an important service since all flours are not alike.

This step, he added, was followed by the railway men (nowadays, mostly truckers) who brought the sacks to town. These shipments merely dropped off the sacks; a whole host of people had to unload the train cars, stock the warehouses, set the flour on the shelves, and finally sell it to customers. The Mystery Chef didn't mention that those tens of thousands of men contributing to this ordinary item exterminated millions of wheat-eating mice, sparrows, groundhogs, weevils, beetles, grubs, etc., so that there was flour to sell in the first place.

Annoyingly, flour is but one of six ingredients required to make biscuits, which also require butter, buttermilk, baking powder, salt, and an oven. Now ponder the pathway for baking powder, and try baking pancakes, biscuits or cake without it. Repeat this thought experiment with butter, buttermilk, salt, and gas/electricity. This is why readers were cautioned that the Mystery Chef's cookbook was "explicit," for he offered unsentimental discussions of the origins of that lovely *homard à l'américaine* (this being a hilarious French recipe for lobster, "American style"). To draw a straight line from thousands of poor workers to the blushing crustacean on your plate was in very bad taste. Offensive, really. Hence, "Mystery Chef." No names, so his crude talk wouldn't embarrass his poor mother.

Ethical hunters do not deny these conditions, which some call a "devil's bargain," and others call "real life." Instead, they face them directly, taking legal responsibility for the death of a single wild animal for the purposes of transforming it into venison. In this sense, the hunter is anachronistic because he is a craftsman, participating in a traditional culture that requires a certain degree of innate talent, a lengthy apprenticeship, the mastery of specialized tools, and loyalty to an ethic based on intrinsic values rather than designer labels. On the socioeconomic plane, this is why so many Americans think of hunters as backwards conservatives who cling to outmoded ways. On the cultural plane, however, it also explains why a 2014 survey conducted by the British website FemaleFirst.com revealed that women voted "chef" the sexiest profession for men, in a country where hunting is traditionally practiced by the aristocracy, and many prestigious chefs forage and hunt wild food to serve to their worldly clientele.

Like "hunter," "chef" is an artisanal occupation strongly aligned with male practitioners and deadly weapons. The activity is sexy because it absorbs the dangerous rawness of the real (the whole fish at the dock, the ethnic markets filled with strange fruits, the face-to-face encounter with the stag), and artfully transforms it through the suave refinements of gastronomy (poached trout in lemon sauce, purée of pomegranate, herb-encrusted medallions of venison). The social value of their masculine practitioners resides in their ability to pivot between two worlds: one wild, the other tame.

× ON THE IMPORTANCE OF KNOWING WHAT YOU'RE TRYING TO ACCOMPLISH

Christopher McCandless, the young man who undertook a misguided quest to get away from civilization by fleeing to Alaska, ended up accomplishing exactly the opposite by ultimately infiltrating every mall in America. Unprepared for the rigors of an Alaskan winter, McCandless died, but the story of his brief life became Jon Krakauer's bestselling book, *Into the Wild*, and then a successful Hollywood film. As romantic as his fate may seem to college kids living in their parents' basement, his death was pointless. Alaskans knew immediately that McCandless had no chance of surviving in the backcountry, for he was underequipped, inexperienced, and had such poor knowledge of woodcraft that he couldn't tell the difference between two large wild animals that, if correctly hunted, butchered, and preserved, could have ensured his survival. "There's a big difference between a moose and a caribou," hunter Gordon Samuel told Krakauer. "A real big difference. You'd have to be pretty stupid not to be able to tell them apart."

It was on a moose hunt that Samuel stumbled onto McCandless's frozen body. A few years later, Samuel ended up shot dead by Alaska state troopers, making headlines as that guy from *Into the Wild* who found himself in a drunken car chase through that town where Sarah Palin used to be mayor. The chain of events leading up to Samuel's death was inexorable if not inevitable, which was true of McCandless's unhappy end as well. But if Samuel's death in Wasilla was unambiguous and swift, McCandless died alone in the woods, and it's still unclear what happened. In 2013, Krakauer provided an update regarding McCandless's cause of death, providing a rather fascinating account of his attempts to prove that the culprit was wild potato seeds. But why was McCandless eating these seeds in the first place? Ingesting wild plants of any kind without *deep* local knowledge is such a risky proposition that most wilderness manuals written by people with years of practice, such as Mykel Hawke, author of the *Green Beret Survival Manual,* advise strongly against it. The larger point is that our brooding hero seemed to have

Comparison of different members of the Cervid family, 19th century.
Credit: Wellcome Institute.

been trying to recover a state of primitive purity, seeking to live out a life somehow better than a dystopian future with a For Sale sign on every corner. But even when he was physically in the woods, his head was still in the suburbs.

It is a common phenomenon. Hence, the dream of Returning to the Forest is worth examining here because bits of it tend to find their way into the current interest in foraging and hunting among disenchanted urbanites, tangling with motives and muddying the task at hand. As far as I'm concerned, this task is not to escape modern life or fight inner demons, but to feed oneself off the fat of the land. To succeed, the head must be in the same place as the feet.

For seasoned hunters, "one shot, one kill" is both a hunting philosophy and a culinary imperative. To accept this blunt claim means dispensing with the image of naked warriors running after their supper. These deer always seem to be bounding through the dappled woods as sunshine beams through canopies of green, and heaven holds its breath as the hunter draws back his string and … zing! The arrow flies straight and true, and so the deer falls. Naturally, there is no blood.

These clichés inform the 18th-century British image on the following page of a "Brazilian" tribesman hunting with bow and arrow. With one well-placed shot, a "Brazilian" hunter has taken down a bird in flight. The hunter is male, young, hale, and healthy, surrounded by rejoicing women and flourishing coconut trees. This image is not unique. There are many more like it, all conveying variations of the same theme, telling the story that long ago, man flourished in a state of primitive simplicity, using weapons he crafted himself, living in nature and feeding himself and his family off the bountiful land. The two standing figures are secular Adam and Eve in an Eden so forgiving that they didn't even need to bring modesty.

Amplify this image a hundred times, via television shows and films where "Indians" on horseback are hunting deer with bow and arrow, and it becomes easy to recognize

A Brasilian

Awnsham Churchill, John Churchill, John Locke, and John Nieuhoff.
A collection of voyages and travels, some now first printed from original manuscripts, others now first published in English, 3rd edition,
London: Printed by assignment from Messrs. Churchill, for H. Lintot
[etc.], 1744 – 46, Plate 1. Credit: Wellcome Institute.

the persistence of certain myths linked to hunting. The latest entry is Katniss Everdeen in *The Hunger Games*, who shoots rabbits from a hundred yards with a recurve bow. This sort of nonsense makes it seem that a bow hunter could pick off a small flying target and still be left with meat to eat once it landed in his loin-cloth. Or, in Katniss's case, her pouch. Thus, the method seems less cruel, more authentic, and therefore better than using rifles, shotguns, or, heaven forfend, an AR-15. Shouldn't today's hunters stick to bow and arrow, then, since the rule, "one shot, one kill," clearly worked using this simple weapon? Err, no. Unfortunately, what Katniss actually represents is a set of myths regarding the "Noble Savage." Same goes for the "Brazilians" in this British image. The problem with such myths is that these particular savages aren't so noble. They're cannibals. The haunch twirling on the spit is a human leg, and one of the bones cast off from their ghastly lunch is a human skull.

Just to be clear: Eighteenth-century South American tribespeople were not cannibals. They worried that the European explorers invading their territory were man-eaters coming to roast *them* for supper. Despite the factual inaccuracies that anthropologists have energetically refuted regarding the culinary quirks of Catholic missionaries, the nagging belief persists that somewhere in the Amazons, relentless men with strange haircuts go hunting for gullible humans to throw into hellfire and brimstone. For similar reasons, the belief also persists that it's easy to bring down a flying bird using a hand-strung bow with homemade arrows with stone tips, and that roasting meat over a spit is a great way to prepare large cuts for a feast. In reality, it's exceptionally difficult to shoot a bird in flight using a bow and arrow; and roasting over a spit is a terrible method of cooking wild meat.

When early English and European explorers crossed the ocean to experience the North American woods, they weren't tourists hoping to sample the local cuisine. They were on a mission for the Pope and the Hudson's Bay Company. There were no roads, no restaurants, and no prepackaged food. They trekked with the assumption there would be fresh wildlife to keep their bellies full. They hunted along the way, seemingly without much preparation and with great confidence that the Lord would provide. However, they had a few things in their favor, starting with the fact that there were 5 billion fewer humans on the planet and a great deal more wildlife. Many explorers died horribly en route, but we remember the fortunate ones who not only survived their ambitious treks but wrote memoirs about them. These men include Hanbury but also Samuel Hearne, George Back, Warburton Pike, John Hornby, J. B. Tyrell, and others whose remarkable accounts of trekking as far as the Arctic Circle deserve to be rescued from obscurity. When they did make it across "the Barrens" and other difficult terrains without obvious forage, they typically did so with the repeated help of indigenous peoples who rescued them when they got in trouble.

They got in trouble a lot. Hanbury, for instance, described Canada as a "land of plenty" where, in spots, there were so many deer that they didn't need to be hunted: they just walked right up to his tent and practically leaped into his stewpot. During leaner times, he noted, something good to eat always turned up—a wolverine, a "fat wolf," ptarmigan, geese, plenty of fish, and musk ox. Things were going pretty well until the canoe got caught in the rapids of the Lockhart River and floated away. They recovered the canoe, but he and his party lost all of their tools, including axes, rifles, guns, and nets.

> We were now without the means of procuring food, and were in the middle of a very rough country. Deer were plentiful, and stood stupidly staring at us within easy range, fish were leaping in the pools on the river, but the means of killing deer or taking fish were gone. Not an enviable position in which to find one's self.

Though they had decades of firsthand experience and a wealth of accumulated knowledge, they had nothing to hunt with and no tools to make basic weapons. They didn't try to make their own bows and arrows because they knew better than to waste energy trying. For six days, he and his party survived by foraging cranberries and blueberries, which are safe to consume because they're easy to recognize and unmistakable at first taste. They did not attempt to eat wild potatoes or their seeds, elderberries, rhubarb, acorns, or other partly edible, partly poisonous plants. Berries were enough to keep them going until they were rescued by a tribe called the Yellow Knives. The Yellow Knives fed them, then sent them on their way with dried meat. Resupplied at the next outpost, the group was none the worse for wear, and so the trek continued.

By the end of their expedition, after a year and a half of moving across the woods, they were completely accustomed to a diet that was wholly wild. Their hunts and catches extended over a range of species that Hanbury and his group had never tried before but found surprisingly palatable. To avoid rabbit starvation, they ate *all* the organs plus the blood and the marrow. To obtain greens, they ate the stomach contents of the ruminants they hunted. Arriving at Fort Normal, which was the end of the story, Hanbury and his men were seated at a table for a "civilized" meal of bread and butter, potatoes, bacon, and the like, the first of such a meal in twenty months. To a man, the entire group ended up with a "severe case of indigestion." It took them a week to readjust to farmed food.

The unhappy condition of the group's intestines challenges the easy assumption that the blandness of cultivars is superior to digesting a wolverine. Just as tellingly, Hanbury found himself wistful for life in the woods. He was able to gloss over the lean portions of his trek because, as he admitted cheerfully, he tended to view his excursions through rose-colored glasses. It was also because he'd known that he wasn't alone in the wilderness. Indeed, he had such confidence in the goodwill and hunting skills of various indigenous tribes that he included a dictionary appendix of English words and phrases in Inuit. In this regard, Hanbury's account matches the others regarding the best way to survive harsh and grueling terrain, including trying to paddle across a lake that was still frozen in July. It's not by going solo, sulking under a tree, or beating your chest and howling at the moon. It's by making friends with the people who *live there*. For years and decades and centuries. If McCandless had bothered to learn from Alaskans who'd grown up in the backwoods, he might have lived to write his own book about his adventures.

× CHOOSE YOUR LOCATION

Hanbury had the good sense to be humble. He called himself a "traveler," knowing full well that the Inuit and other peoples had lived in the Arctic Circle for thousands of years and weren't impressed by him. There are more than a few lessons in his adventure, not the least of which is this: all hunting is local, and the plants and animals got there long before you. So did a whole lot of people who think living without gas or electricity is normal.

Hunting begins and ends with the land. The wild animal is part of the land, bound and obedient to nature's laws. The kind of hunters who write books about the experience are usually just visiting—and not in a metaphysical, "we're all just guests of Mother Earth" kind of way, but as shiny strangers in a new place. Hanbury called the hunting he was doing "sport," because he arrived in North America knowing that he was going to leave. A twenty-month trip seems long to us, but it wasn't long to him. He and his group practiced a nineteenth-century version of eating fast food on the road, prioritizing speed and convenience, filling empty stomachs while anticipating there would be a place to grab food when they got hungry again. They selected their meals based on the wildlife that was immediately present, making do with ptarmigans in hand instead of holding out for more familiar fare, like pigeons. The "where" of their journey determined what they ate.

Hanbury hunted deer when herds were handy because he knew what to expect, how to dress it out, how to prep it for supper, and more or less how it would taste.

"There They Are," c. 1874–1880, from "Sketches of Hudson Bay life," (album) by H. Bullock Webster 1874–1880 collection. Credit: UBC library.

He also hunted and fished everything else that came within range, including hares and birds. At one point, he scavenged a deer carcass half-eaten by a predator. He began by accepting the land's non-negotiable conditions, which included feeding himself based on what was already there, rather than expecting to change it to suit his tastes. This is not to say that the Hudson's Bay Company was full of bleeding-heart environmentalists counting butterflies and measuring tree rings. It was a bunch of profit-minded fur traders who took over great chunks of Canada so it could exploit the natural resources. But on the individual plane, Hanbury and his group hunted for food, and his comments reveal a certain wonder at the unfamiliar ease of that undertaking in the Great Northern Woods.

Hanbury's catch-as-catch-can approach to provisioning must be fully appreciated, as it is alien to current sensibilities where breakfast, lunch, and supper not only correspond to dawn, noon, and sunset, but are coordinated to the institutionalized schedules of the school day and the workplace. Nowadays, it's common to refer to snacking throughout the day as "grazing," as if M & M's plucked randomly from glass candy dishes is akin to a ruminant grazing on the grass. But what is far more "natural" is food insecurity. When is the next bit of nutritional energy coming? From nut, seed, or bug?

To hunt and forage from a platform of uncertainty is the opposite of grocery shopping and trophy hunting, both of which affirm political and economic power over another country's natural resources. As an extension of colonialist practices, 19th-century British big game hunters would travel to India, with the express purpose of hunting tigers, elephants, and other large animals not present on English country estates. Instead of staying long enough to study the animals and learn the terrain, they would hire local guides who possessed this intimate information. Today, guided hunting persists because of the scarcity principle, chiefly lack of time. In an hourly-rate world, ordinary people can't afford to devote years to studying the wildlife and scouting for signs, and so pay others to guide them into unfamiliar terrains. These opportunities are not cheap: a recently advertised weeklong guided caribou hunt in Ontario—nothing fancy, just basic cabins and fireplace food—costs $8,000 American dollars, not including airfare or secondary tags for small game. Regular people save up years for the opportunity. Because of the sums involved, this kind of focus transforms the animal into a fetish. By contrast, subsistence hunting focuses on transforming the carcass into venison.

Land-based hunting is characterized by generational hunting, and often on tribal or family land. It is also not only regional but local in the most literal sense, or practiced inside a locality that imposes its conditions on you, in the manner of frozen ground or arid sand. Yelling at the snow doesn't make it stop falling, and crying in the desert won't make grass grow. Polar bears don't thrive in Florida, and reindeer can't survive in France. In the United States, one of the most adaptable species happens to be whitetail deer, which thrive in grasslands, forests, cold weather, warm weather, and they love living in the suburbs. But they are so attached to cornfields that the *Total Deer Hunting Manual* by the editors of *Field and Stream* designated "farmland" as a habitat. In brief, certain generalizations can be made about best hunting practices for your region, but the details that spell success can only come from someone who's spent a long time studying the quarry as a living extension of the particular parcel of land you're hunting.

Consider, then, that you'd like to practice traditional hunting, and you've decided to focus on deer for the purpose of putting meat on the table. Perhaps you are also hunting in order to improve self-sufficiency, to obtain quality meat, or simply want to master a traditional skill. How, exactly, do you go about starting? Given that we need guidebooks to shop for fresh vegetables on store shelves, what happens when there's no store and the Meat section refuses to stand still? The first challenge for new hunters is access to land where wildlife can be legally hunted. Bambi may be munching on your blueberry bushes every night, but no, you cannot shoot him even assuming that it's deer season, and you're licensed to hunt with a tag for the season and have a loaded shotgun handy. Hunting is banned in the suburbs because there are too many obstacles getting in the way. Hence the first hunt that hunters must undertake is the one for a hunting ground where there are no houses, no dogs, and no humans.

Wildlife lives in the wild. It also wanders into backyards,

but proximity to human residences means that it's off limits to hunting. The lay of the land not only determines if hunting is legal in your town/county/state/region/country/continent in the first place, but also dictates what kind of hunting can be practiced, and which genre of weapons can be used. Bow hunting v. shotgun v. rifle v. muzzleloader is not only a personal preference, but also contingent on the neighborhood, the terrain, and the seasons. Legal restrictions cast different light on the American deer population statistics, for it is often stated that they've rebounded to about the same numbers as they were during Colonial times. However, large numbers of these deer are crowding into the Northeast corridor. They are so populous and regionally distinct that they constitute their own subgroup, called the Northern whitetail. This portion of the United States is prime residential and urban real estate, and broad swaths of these areas are not huntable because there are too many humans getting in the way. When the deer are hanging out at the mall, they're not game. They're loiterers, and so the police are called to shoo them away.

In other words, the deer are crowding into areas where hunters cannot hunt. It seems that deer, too, enjoy the amenities of living in a community where there's good roads, clean water, and lots of easily accessible food. Thus, while it seems to nonhunters as if getting a deer is as simple as throwing a rock at one, hunters have to go where people are not.

The problem of accessing huntable land is rarely mentioned in books about hunting. Nonetheless, it is an increasing challenge for hunters of all kinds. American dreamer McCandless went to Alaska. Danish baroness Dinesen traveled to Africa, and British explorer Hanbury traveled to northern Canada and the Arctic Circle. In other words, all of them were hunting so far from their own backyards that they ended up hunkering down in different time zones. If you are an ordinary person with a job, or even half a job, where do you go to hunt if your family doesn't own a forest? Writes Joel MacCharles of the Canadian website and blog WellPreserved.ca: "If you want to learn to hunt and don't know anyone here [in Ontario] who has, there are significant barriers to enter that are largely divided into cost, knowledge and access." These three things are inseparable from each other. "If you don't have knowledge or access to land," he notes, "your cost of entry is going to be massive." Like, say, US $8,000, which I consider a lot of money, even if the takeaway is a couple hundred pounds of caribou meat. From the standpoint of time and money, those trips are unsustainable.

In order to hunt deer, in other words, the first step is to hunt for a place free of humans but full of wildlife. Where you go is entirely dependent on your region, your free time, your budget, your age, stamina, and fitness. The first resource to check is the US Department of Fish and Wildlife, which will direct you to public lands where deer hunting is permitted during hunting season. (Whitetail hunting is not year-round. In the United Kingdom, by contrast, its six species are hunted at different times of the year.) There is no one place to hunt, and every terrain is distinct. Patches of forest can tuck into corners of developed land, and deer can live in areas surrounded by skyscrapers.

Increasingly difficult to access, the wild is both a place and a concept, both of which are increasingly remote from everyday experience. More than anything else, however, hunting for venison is a mindset. It's not that the opportunities aren't there. It's that you have to view the land as your food source, which means putting yourself in the deer's place by following its paths. The land, the deer, the hunter, in that order. Reverse it, and it's not hunting. It's farming.

CHAPTER TWO
The Hunter and the Quarry

"One does not hunt in order to kill; on the contrary, one kills in order to have hunted," Jose Ortega Y Gasset famously observed in *Meditations on Hunting*, first published in 1972. In its purest form, the kill not only marks the completion of the hunt but is its defining element. That fatal shot distills the hunt down to a single moment, proclaiming: "I have shot it, it is dead, and now the hunt is done." At this point, the story ends, and there is much rejoicing.

That's nice, but what happened to the venison?

In real life, it can take years to get to the point where the hunter can take a shot at a legal buck. These years are usually left out of hunting stories, because the acquisition of woodcraft skills doesn't translate well into words, and no hunter wants to give away details regarding a piece of huntable land they've spent years walking. This is the "appren-

Currier and Ives, "The Death Shot," 1870-1880, Library of Congress.

ticeship" phase of traditional hunting, which is distinguished here from canned hunts—called "canned" because they're artificial. Because they guarantee a kill at the end of the day, they're ethically identical to going to the grocery store and buying your food.

For subsistence hunters, the shot is the end of one phase and the beginning of another: cooking. When hunting for the express purpose of obtaining meat for the table, the goal is to quickly and efficiently down your quarry in the manner that respects its life as a fully wild being. The most respectful manner is a "clean" death that comes very swiftly. As it happens, this swift death also results in better venison. Not only is there an intimate connection between the health of the animal and the fullness of the land, but also between the edibility of the venison and the hunter's shooting skills. A wild animal's flesh is a record of its life in the wild. As it browses on berries, corn, or acorns, the deer is infused with these same flavors. But even a coddled deer that spent its entire life being hand-fed and pampered will make terrible eating if it's been chased for hours.

This affirmation can be confusing, as popular culture reinforces the myth that hunters literally chase after their quarry, whether by running noiselessly through the woods, or riding bareback on galloping pintos as they shoot arrow after arrow into their running targets. In real life, this doesn't happen. As appealing as these energetic visions may be, everyday hunting used to look more like this image from Frenchman Samuel de Champlain's book chronicling his travels in Canada, published in 1619.

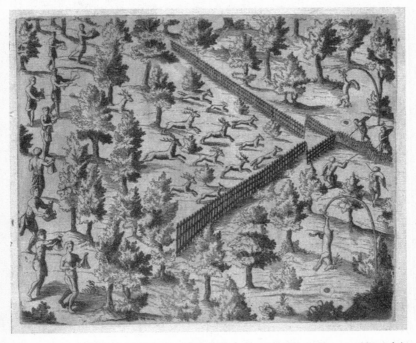

Bird's-eye view of a Native American deer hunt in New France (Canada), showing Indians driving deer toward fences into a narrow enclosure to be killed, and two dead deer hanging from bent trees, wood engraving, [1619], from Voyages et descouvertures faites en la Nouvelle France, depuis l'année 1615 ... / Samuel de Champlain. Paris:C. Collet, 1619, opp. p. 52. LoC.

At the extreme left, a line of "Indians" are driving a herd of deer into a fenced area that narrows into a trap. On the other side of the trap, men holding spears are waiting to deal the fatal blow to the deer. Behind them, two bucks are already killed, dressed, and hanging from saplings. Europeans also practiced this method of driving deer. As shown by this image produced at the same time that Champlain was "discovering" New France (i.e., Canada), European nobles used dogs to drive herds of deer into nets, where men armed with spears waited at the ready.

Jan van der Straet, Hunting: dogs scare the deer into nets, whilst a hunter throws his spear into the antlers of a stag. Engraving by Philipp Galle after Stradanus, c. 1600. Credit: Wellcome Institute.

On royal hunts where the quarry was not driven into nets or stakes, the stag could be "coursed" (chased) for days by packs of hunting dogs and nobles on horseback, such as the two that appear in the upper left corner of van der Straet's engraving. The hunting dogs are greyhounds, originally bred for the necessary speed and stamina to keep up with horses and stags. These hounds were an integral part of the hunt—but they were not "the hunter." Neither were the men holding the spears, for only royals had the right to hunt. Nobles possessed land. Peasants did not. Though others participated in the hunt, they were not "the hunter," in the same way that guides on weekend hunts possess the knowledge of the land but do not have the rights to the quarry.

By the 17th century in Europe, however, it had become taboo for any hunter to consume a coursed stag. The reasons for this taboo were grounded in Christian symbolism as well as military tradition, but it also reflected the fact that the venison of a coursed stag was inedible. Instead, it became the tradition at the end of every royal hunt for the venison, blood, and entrails to be immediately fed to the dozens of dogs that participated. This practice served the dual purpose of providing the dogs with premium protein, while getting them accustomed to the taste of venison as part of their training. On occasion, the venison from one of the royal hunts would be offered to peasants, who would reject the gamy stuff in disgust, insulted that they were being offered dog food.

For early explorers, by contrast, as well as indigenous peoples living chiefly off wild food, the tradeoff between hunting deer to survive, and putting up with the terrible taste, was a choice they constantly had to face. When Hanbury found himself in the entrance to the Chesterfield Inlet near the mouth of the Kazan River on July 12, he was surprised to find the river frozen, and so he was forced to make camp for five days.

> Deer, although fairly plentiful, were very difficult to get near, owing to the plague of mosquitoes, which was now at its height, but I managed always to kill enough for our immediate use. The flesh of the deer at this time was hardly fit to eat, being discoloured all through. The marrow, usually a luxury, was now of the consistency of blood and water, owing to the

"fly-time," the wretched beasts being kept on the run day and night.

A deer that is being "pushed" will not taste good. In his *Journey from the Prince of Wales's Fort in Hudson Bay to the Northern Ocean in the Years 1769, 1770, 1771, and 1772,* first published in 1795, explorer Samuel Hearne made similar observations regarding deer and moose that he'd helped to chase through deep snow some forty years before Hanbury arrived to chronicle his adventures. The native Indians would chase the quarry to the point of exhaustion, at which point it could be killed with a knife. However, Hearne commented, the venison was "very disagreeable" in taste and "clammy" in texture. But the reason he complained a lot about the venison was because he had little choice but to chomp his way through it.

Both Hearne and Hanbury were chasing deer through the snow, making them "winter" deer even if, in Hanbury's case, it was the middle of July. These deer would have been lean from months of erratic access to browse. This leanness would have made their meat difficult to choke down even if the deer had been dropped where they stood. The stress of living in harsh winter conditions created the "discoloration" in the venison, but it was the "fly-time" that ruined it definitively. Whether running away from annoying mosquitos or hungry hunters, these deer were not calmly munching on corn and basking in the sunlit grass, but eking out an existence off a land of ice and snow.

When a deer is pushed for any length of time, the stress negatively affects the venison. Running pumps blood and lactic acid into the muscles, potentially infusing the entire animal with a "gamy" taste. But it's not just lactic acid that injures the taste. Running legs require energy. The reason why exercise prompts heavy breathing is because this helps raise the level of oxygen in the blood. This is aerobic exercise, or exercise with oxygen. When this effort isn't enough, an anaerobic process called glycolysis kicks in. Without requiring additional oxygen, glycolysis initiates a breakdown of sugars that leads to the production of lactate. Energy levels surge temporarily. On the downside, high lactate levels increase the acidity of the muscle cells and disrupt other metabolic processes, causing that burning sensation in muscles being pushed past their usual limits.

In effect, the muscle is not only filled with lactic acid but it is also damaged on the cellular level, filled with micro tears that provoke a "repair" response. It takes a few days for the inflamed muscle tissue to return to a calm state, days that the quarry does not have. If the hunter finally manages to drop the pushed deer and preps it for dinner, every bite will force the diner to taste a litany of its woes. Because meat is muscle, a stressed deer makes bad venison, which ends up being both mushy-tough in texture, and strong and bitter in taste. A recital of its last moments on earth.

× **THE SHOT**

These effects are separate and distinct from the consequences of a badly placed shot. A bad shot is one that merely wounds. It does not immediately kill the quarry, which then leaps away, obliging the hunter to run after it. A wounded deer, trailed for yards or miles, will not be good eating. Not only will it be saturated with stress hormones, the wound itself is damaged tissue that must be trimmed out, and it might be days before it falls. Then the hunter has to find it, by which time it may be already decomposing. In order to avoid this dismal prospect, responsible hunters choose the correct weapon for their quarry, and practice until they're crack shots. Though some hunters prefer crossbow or bow and arrow, the vast majority of hunters rely on firearms as the most practical weapon for deer hunting.

There are entire books devoted to the single subject of choosing the best firearm for deer hunting. For example, Laurence Koller's *Shots at Whitetails*, 1948, is a weighty tome republished several times and still worth reading. He divides deer hunters into five groups:

a) Men new to hunting with no shooting experience except plinking in the backyard with a .22
b) Men new to deer hunting but with some experience hunting small game with a shotgun
c) Experienced hunters who moved to the city and only get out their guns once or twice a year
d) Target shooters who can handle still targets but have no woodcraft or hunting skills
e) The lifelong woodsmen and hunters, who treat their own rifle like "a warm, personal friend."

To which I would add, f) Men and women new to hunting with no shooting experience—a creature that Koller couldn't imagine in 1948. He goes into the details of rifles, shotguns, calibers, and other factors related to using a firearm for deer hunting, stressing that the novice hunter has to first overcome the hurdle of mastering a firearm before any form of hunting can be ventured. But as far as finding the perfect firearm is concerned, Koller repeats that there is no one size that fits all, and the preferred weapon will change as novices acquire skills and learn their limits as well as the habits of the quarry.

Personal preference trumps conventional wisdom every time, for your primary concern should not be what "everybody" uses, but what weapon you can handle which is also an appropriate caliber for your quarry. This being said, the general consensus is that the classic deer hunting rifle is a Winchester .30-30, model 94. This is the model that your grandma and grandpa used, and many hunters still swear by it. In the past fifty years or so, the Winchester .270 has taken over as the trusty standard deer hunting rifle. In the mid-20th century, a professional hunter named Jack Conner settled on the Winchester .270 as the ideal deer rifle, and a lot of hunters since then have agreed with him. This bolt-action rifle is a high velocity weapon that shoots flat with great accuracy out to three hundred yards. In the hands of a hunter who shoots with consistency, this rifle ensures that a deer can drop in its tracks with a single, well-placed shot. The deer dies without knowing it's dead. No wasting ammo, no wasting meat, and no cruelty.

1. If the weapon is too heavy, the meat will be "shot-up" and no good. This problem is compounded when the wrong ammo is used. "Shot-up" means exactly that: it's meat that has been pulverized by the bullet's impact. It can create a trail of internal destruction that leaves behind a bloody mess. Shot-up venison cannot be salvaged and ground up for burgers (I've tried). It's a good way to lose meat, and a common error of first-time hunters.

2. Conversely, however, if the weapon is too light (a .22 Crickett, for example), the deer will not drop in its tracks. Wounded, it may disappear back into its habitat, never to be found. It may survive, and often does. But it may not. Either way, it means the hunt is a failure.

3. If the overexcited hunter shoots multiple rounds into the deer, the meat will be too damaged to salvage. This is a variation of the first problem, using ammo that's too heavy. It's also a function of not understanding deer biology: a well- placed shot to the heart means the deer is dead but it will not necessarily drop immediately. Due to the adrenaline surge, which is far more powerful in deer than in humans, it may take a few seconds, even minutes, before it falls. Hunters that do not trust their skills just keep shooting, once again producing shot-up venison that will be mostly inedible.

4. If the shot is not well placed, the deer will suffer. The worst of bad shots is "paunching" the deer. A disaster, as a gut shot pierces the intestines, wounding but not killing the deer, and tainting its meat with urine and fecal matter. Unless you are desperate, it's generally undesirable to consume meat that's been contaminated this way. You are sad, your hungry family is mad, and the deer is dead, all for nothing.

Solution?
1. Find the most appropriate weapon for your hunt that you can also handle comfortably, and practice until you're expert with it.
2. Match the ammo to the quarry, using the lightest load possible to get the job done.
3. Learn to stay calm. (This is much more difficult than it seems.)
4. Know what part of the anatomy to aim for, and don't miss.

× **WHAT IS A QUARRY, ANYWAY?**

I've been using the term "quarry" as if it's synonymous with deer. However the term refers to prey in general, and the hunter chasing them isn't necessarily human. It originally referred to game hunted with hawks. The word itself is a modification of the Middle English *quire*, also *querre*, referring to the entrails (which eventually became the entire animal) given to the hounds at the end of a successful hunt. When the royals hunted, the quarry was not any mature buck that happened to be around, but a specific stag selected by the Master of the Hunt as the most impressive specimen.

For centuries, the royal hunt focused intently on the stag as the quarry, and a stag that was coursed by the king always had a ten-point rack. Anything less was not worthy. This legacy has had a lasting impact. The British colonists who settled in New England weren't nobles, but they retained the hunt's traditional focus on a mature male deer with the most impressive antlers. This is not to say that younger, immature, or female deer weren't hunted too. They just weren't celebrated or commemorated, because they were hunted as food.

Today, to preferentially hunt smaller, younger deer today requires explanation, as it strikes many as odd and even wrong to pass up the buck with the large rack. The ease of hunting younger animals still contributes to their low status on the prestige totem pole. Unlike mature stags, young females don't present the threat of lethal violence, and so the hunter isn't physically or psychologically challenged. This disappointment only makes sense if the hunter-quarry relationship can be understood as a battle of strength, wit, stamina, and skill, instead of one step in a sustained culinary operation that also provides necessary sustenance. It is also the case that Americans are conditioned to think of does as being off limits, as a result of widespread hunting bans initiated in the 1930s to protect whitetails, the populations of which had dropped precipitously due to unregulated over-hunting and loss of habitat between the Wars. Since then the whitetail has rebounded so dramatically that it's now a nuisance animal in certain regions. Correspondingly, hunting restrictions have considerably loosened, and doe tags are now available in limited quantities.

In previous centuries, the idea of hunting does failed to produce even the tiniest shudder of horror, so the fact that it strikes us as being wrong is a function of other social and cultural factors, including the fact that red meat in American grocery stores is supposed to be male, from the veal (male calf) to the steak (castrated bull). Yet to prioritize a tender doe over a trophy buck not only contributes to the happiness of the table, it also serves the health of the herd. Inside an undisturbed and balanced ecosystem, animal predators such as eagles and wolves target sick animals as well as smaller, weaker juveniles and females. But well-intentioned humans reason that females and juveniles must be given a chance to replenish the herd—in the lifeboat, it's women and children first—and it's unchivalrous to consider otherwise. As a result, both sport and subsistence hunting traditionally emphasize impressive mature males as the quarry while largely exempting juveniles and females.

Recently, a group of scientists researched the effects of this practice on the bighorn Dall sheep, and concluded that the average sheep is shrinking in size because the smaller, less aggressive males have been given opportunities to breed, ultimately weakening the entire species' chances of long-term survival in the wild. By restricting hunting to large males in the interests of sport and fairness, in other words, human laws are "actually selecting in a direction that is opposite to what natural selection would be," noted lead scientist Marco Festa-Biachet regarding the 2013 study's findings.

Nowadays, in the West, the stress on the mature male as the quarry is so ingrained that it's even difficult to persuade subsistence hunters that their venison will be far better if they go for the youngster. In a recent issue of *Fur Fish and Game*, a first-person account of a "meat moose hunt" written by an Alaskan woman named Miki Collins illuminates the issues. Like many Alaskans who live in "the bush," she grew up in a household that relied on wild meat to survive, and yet it took her several years of hunting on her own to figure out that a young bull was much better eating than an old bull. "I'll never forget peering through a screen of brush and being startled by a tender two-year-old peering back … Mighty good eating, he was." She now chooses the young bull moose as her quarry, passing over the "tough" trophy bulls and serving her stomach rather than feeding her ego. "Some think they know all about moose," she concludes. "Not me. As I head into my 33rd year [of moose hunting], I do so confident that I'll learn something new."

× **GETTING IN PLACE**

In order to avoid chasing the deer around, experienced hunters invest a great deal of time figuring out where they're liable to go, and then doing everything in their power to get there first. It's illegal to bait deer, trap deer, or use dogs, and just because you saw a deer calmly munching on apples in the same spot for three days in a row doesn't mean that it will be there tomorrow. It may have eaten all the apples, and moved on to a new orchard. It can be very frustrating, which is why traditional hunting requires prep work and scouting. This prep work makes it possible to predict where the deer like to browse, so the hunter can be in place and waiting for them to show up, rather than spotting them from afar and chasing after them.

In 1830, Peter Hawker's *Instructions to Young Sportsmen* gave this pragmatic advice: If a hunter is lying in wait and a deer is standing in profile, shoot it in the neck or the head. A deer facing you directly is the "worst," but when the deer is standing still with its buttocks toward you, try to shoot it at the base of the skull. If you are a bad shot, but the deer are eating all your crops,

> go out in a summer morning just after sunrise, while the dew is on the grass, or un-ripe corn, and look with caution into every enclosure, and particularly among young peas. You must be very silent, because, if a buck hears you, he will probably lie down so close as to escape your notice; but, if you go carefully and silently, you will see him feeding.

To keep the deer from catching wind of your scent, Hawker advises that you carry an armful of sweet hay in front of you.

In other words, for a hunter lying in wait who is facing a deer positioned broadside and calmly feeding on corn, the best shot is an instantly lethal shot to the deer's head or neck. However, this shot should only be tried by those skilled enough to hit a very small moving target. The advice remains the same today. Improvements in gun technology notwith-standing, a head shot is tricky. Thus, the most experienced hunters try instead for the heart/lungs, which is a safer shot and also a very effective placement though it sacrifices the heart—a gastronomic treat for some.

Pragmatically, Hawker points out that lots of hunters are lousy marksmen who are lucky to hit any part of the deer. To make up for that deficiency, they must get very close to their target, a task that requires stealth and scent blockers. Hawker isn't being judgmental here; he's just being realis-tic about the fact that hunters possess disparate levels of shooting skills and must compensate by fooling their quarry. Armed with "a pretty stout gun, loaded with a mixture of mould and A or B shot," the bad marksman is still liable to botch the situation, Hawker comments. Instead of managing a clean shot, he will merely wound the deer, which will thus keep on running at full speed, quite possibly charging straight at the hapless hunter before it disappears into a thicket.

One of three spots will drop a calm deer: head, heart, and neck. A hit in any other part of the anatomy has un-foreseeable consequences, including getting run over by the quarry. Interestingly, a head shot will ruin the suitability of the head as a wall-mounted trophy but produces the best re-sults in terms of the quality of the venison. For this reason, a skilled hunter lucky enough to be tracking a herd of deer must decide between a trophy for the wall, or best food for the table, and that choice informs every step of the hunt from the kind of ammo employed, to the cuts used when skinning.

If a magnificent 10-point buck is resting calmly next to a fat young spikehorn, which one is your quarry? In Jan van der Straet's engraving from 1600, this is the choice faced by the hunter lying in wait by a field where cattle are grazing. The group has set up a decoy bull and shooting from behind it. That this "bull" is actually a hunting blind is revealed by its unusual skirt, which opens in front to reveal the bent knee and boot of the hunter hiding inside it.

Jan van der Straet, Hunters hiding behind cattle and horse carts to avoid being seen by the deer they are aiming at, c. 1600. Credit: Wellcome Institute.

The hunter is in position to take a clear shot at a 10-point buck that is broadside to him and bedded down by the water, as well as the spikehorn standing right next to him. From a culinary perspective, the choice is obvious. Young adults of both sexes make the best eating, if taken at their peak seasons. In the domestic meat industry, it is understood that the age of the cow, chicken, and pig directly impacts the texture of the meat, just as its diet affects its flavor and fattiness. The meat will taste like what the animal has been eating, because fat cells will store any fat-soluble materials from its diet, with these flavors concentrating as it gets older. So grass-fed beef tastes of grass, and cows raised on corn and soybeans yield a bland, mildly flavored beef. As animals age, the amount of collagen binding muscle fibers together increases, and the levels of enzymes breaking down proteins decreases. So it tends to be tougher. But for hunters, the more important reason to avoid a mature buck isn't because it is necessarily tougher, but because it is *certainly* more difficult to drop in a single shot and far more liable to start running. These stressed bucks are filled with testosterone and bristling with scent glands. Once they're finally dropped and found, they make hunters scowl and complain about the lousy venison.

Thus, the 19th-century *White House Cookbook* recommended young autumn bucks and summer does for best eating. The youngest bucks (around 1.5 years old) are too young for the rut, the annual mating season which suppresses males' appetites and makes them stringy and lean as they run about, so intent on finding love that they forget to eat. Bucks that are slightly older (1.5 – 2 years old) and taken early in the season are also "young" and unlikely to be rutting. Summer does are gearing up for pregnancy and winter and so they are doing their best to turn themselves into walking balls of fat. As it happens, the oldest hunting manuals, which are French and date from the 14th century, also recommended does for the table. Pregnant hinds (the female red deer) and female roe deer, to be exact, for they were fat, tender, and slow. By the 1950s, this advice had modified somewhat but retained the same general parameters. As André L. Simon commented in the *Concise Encylopedia of Gastronomy*, 1952, "The flesh of the male, or buck, is of better flavour than that of the doe, but neither the one nor the other should be over three years old; they are at their best from eighteen months to two years." For seven centuries, in other words, from the 14th century to the present, people who regularly ate wild venison have concluded that young bucks and does are better eating than mature bucks with impressive racks.

If you are fortunate enough to get a tag for a doe or antlerless buck, then, don't apologize for it. Instead, examine the premises that make the "big buck" so desirable to humans, in light of what science now tells us regarding the preferred quarries of wild carnivores who hunt for food alone.

CHAPTER THREE
The Pivot

× **BLOOD AND GUTS**

The deer is down. Dropped in its tracks, it died a good death. The shot was clean, right through the neck. The deer is young, plump, and appears to be healthy. Now what?

The most skilled and dedicated hunters manage to achieve optimal results on a consistent basis, and justifiably take pride in them. It is also the case that luck and skill are no guarantee of results, and even the most experienced hunters will have to address an imperfect shot, leading to the paunched deer, the lost deer, or the zombie deer that rose up from the dead and nearly killed them. The "dead" deer that goes wandering off is a deer that must be found. Hounds used to be brought in to track the quarry after it had been shot.

Two hunting dogs guarding the carcass of a stag by sitting next to it. Etching by Edward Hacker after C. B. Spalding. London: Rogerson & Tuxford, 1859. Credit: Wellcome Institute.

Without them, a difficult job gets more difficult. Wounded, the quarry will eventually fall, but the search for its body can go on for hours and even days. This length of time isn't a terrible problem if the temps are hovering around freezing and the coyotes aren't sniffing around. It's a disaster for your dinner plans if the weather is warm and there's no snow on the ground.

Conventional wisdom now emphasizes that the quarry must be field dressed as quickly as possible after it expires, so finding a lost deer is a priority if the hunter hopes to save the venison. For best eating, you want to get to the body while it is still fresh. If looking for a wounded deer turns the hunter into a detective searching for blood drops on the grass and interpreting spatter patterns on leaves, field dressing turns the hunter into a medic who needs a basic grasp of anatomy and biology to rescue the downed quarry. Neither step is intuitive; the inability to figure them out is one of the reasons why early humans domesticated dogs and invented cooking. Twentieth-century biologists have given us the reason why the deer must be reached as quickly as possible after death. It has to do with decomposition.

It's a fearful word, decomposition, but along with photosynthesis (that polite process that creates phytonutrients in plants), it anchors every ecosystem. During photosynthesis, plants use light, water, carbon dioxide, energy, and other nutrients as they grow into forests and fields of tasty decidua such as blueberry bushes. Otherwise known as "biomass," these bushes are eaten by deer. Deer are also "biomass," as this is a scientific way of saying "living bulk," and deer biomasses versus plant biomasses are just different states inside a functioning ecosystem. Along comes the hunter, who shoots an appetizing biomass helpfully called a "forkhorn," because its antlers are shaped like forks. Down it goes. Immediately, its stilled heart and deflating lungs tell the cells in its body that it's time to break down. The body begins losing internal heat, the cells lose their structural integrity, enzymatic activity begins to attack the muscle tissue, and anaerobic bodies such as bacteria start to proliferate in their newly oxygen-free environment. Within three to six hours, depending on the size of the quarry, rigor mortis sets in. When the decomposition process is complete, the nutrients initially used in photosynthesis are returned back to nonliving state so that they are once again usable to plants. By taking the animal and consuming it, the hunter becomes a direct part of the process of energy conversion inside a particular ecosystem. Thanks to decomposition, the cycle renews itself. Without decomposition, the plants would starve.

When the body is fresh, very little of this process is evident to the nose or the naked eye. The "off" smell that eventually hits the nose is methane (the odor of farts), ammonia, and other gases. The most obvious visible symptom of bacterial decomposition is bloat. If the body smells bad and looks like an overinflated balloon, you're too late to rescue the venison.

Bloat is an accumulation of carbon dioxide and other by-products made by bacteria breaking down internal tissues. Your tongue can taste these cellular implosions, and your bowels will stage a protest. It's better to find the deer with all haste, and avoid the inevitable drama.

× A BRIEF HISTORY OF FIELD DRESSING

It's useful to have a bit of background regarding the practice of field dressing, which is also called "hog dressing," "rough dressing," "woods dressing," and "gutting it out." It's because the process is not obvious that first-timers have such a hard time figuring out the best way to proceed. The first record of field dressing comes from a 13th-century German manuscript of the knight Tristan. In the West, all hunting lore derives from the practices described in this manuscript. In popular culture, Tristan has become the lovestruck boy obsessed with his uncle's wife, Isolde, but the original version contained pages of graphic instructions regarding the best way to dress the quarry.

A temporarily homeless knight royal, Tristan encounters courtly hunters that are dressing out a coursed stag "in the manner of a hog," on its belly with all four legs splayed out. They are preparing to cut it into four equal pieces, literally quartering the animal. He stops them and tells them there is a better way, which begins by flipping the stag on its back. He starts by skinning the stag from under the chin all the way down, then works the skin off the forelegs, followed by the rear legs, and the sides. He cuts off the skinned shoulders at the ribs, then makes a large cut though the midsection and removes both rear legs together, taking the sirloin, the rump roast, and the haunches. Only after he has cut off the flanks and ribs from the back does he bother with the intestines and other viscera, which he refuses to remove himself as this is too indelicate an operation for someone of his social rank. Having created a nice stack made up of "the breast, the shank, and hocks, the flanks," he then fishes the liver and the testicles out of the gut pile and bundles them up as special delicacies reserved for the king. The heart, lungs, and gut are immediately fed to the hounds. The head, neck, breast, and backbone go "to the poor people."

Combining field dressing, skinning, and butchering, this approach seems rather efficient. No dragging the deer out, no hanging the carcass, no preserving the trophy head or worrying about warm-weather spoilage. Today, however, the conventional order of the operation is reversed: the process starts with the guts, and ends with the skinning; the liver is dog food and the testicles get tossed. What that says about contemporary society is a book in itself, but the takeaway from Tristan's account is the critical importance of working swiftly from start to finish. The hunters didn't need to go searching for the downed quarry because they were chasing it on horseback with hounds. Tristan himself operated so quickly that he startled the men in the group. Whether cut into four equal parts or disassembled according to muscle groups, the quarry never has time to decompose or go into rigor, alleviating that problem from the start. The venison carried back to the castle was so fresh it practically grunted.

× THE NEW FIELD DRESSING

When field dressing starts immediately after downing, improper cooling never arises as a problem. If European knights hunting seven centuries ago weren't thinking about cooling the carcass, the benefits still happened by accident. The combination of field dressing, skinning, and butchering all at one time also headed off the additional buildup of lactic acid preceding rigor mortis. For modern hunters, by contrast, getting the carcass cooled as quickly as possible is a major motivation to reach the downed quarry as quickly as possible and field dress it swiftly. Ambient temperatures around 40°F degrees will slow the growth of bacteria and discourage insect activity.

To start, clear the area of debris and hang hunter's orange around your prep space. Some basic tools of field dressing include a 9" hunting knife, a gutting or gut-hook knife, a container for the liver and heart, some precut 6" pieces of twine, a food-safe rag or roll of paper towels, and some strips of hunter's orange. Before starting, it's helpful to study deer anatomy or any four-footed mammal, really, since they're all pretty similar.

Waterhouse Hawkins, Skeleton of an antelope, with that of a man, who is shown restraining the skeleton of a seated stag by kneeling on the animal's back and holding its antlers. Lithograph, London, 1860. Credit: Wellcome Institute.

Snapping on the disposable plastic gloves, the hunter becomes a forensic pathologist, tracking the symptoms of decomposition as the operation commences. Instead of a scalpel, the tool is a gutting knife, nowadays a hybrid gut-hook knife, and sometimes a gut-hook-skinning knife. A good gutting knife is a worthwhile investment, as this knife makes the task much easier, and it is ideally reserved for this single purpose for purposes of best hygiene.

The deer is on its back. The fur should be full, thick, and glossy. After assessing the entire body from the exterior, inspecting for signs of disease, make a small cut just under the center of the breastbone: pinch a bit of the hide between two fingers, pull it up, and make a small incision in that bit of skin. (If using a gutting knife with a hook, poke the hook into the pinched bit of skin. This kind of knife is sometimes called a "zipper" because the action is akin to unzipping a coat.) Do not stick the knife down into the chest with a stabbing motion, but slide it forward and sideways. Underneath the fur and the skin is a thin wall of muscle, so there will be resistance. Push the knife slowly until there is no more resistance. Then stop.

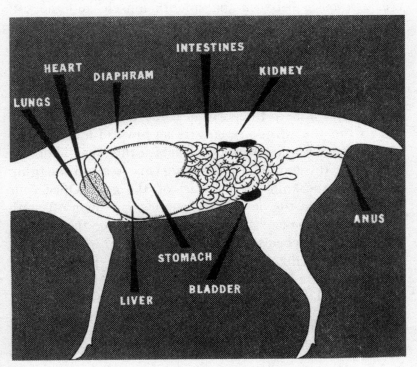

Diagram of deer's internal organs, from *The Venison Book*, 1954.

The reason for starting at the breastbone is this: there is bone underneath. By starting at this point, you can be reasonably sure that your knife will not pierce the peritoneal sac, the membrane that holds the viscera together. The piercing of the sac is not a problem, in and of itself, but it increases the likelihood that the knife will accidentally puncture the intestines or, if you start at the other end, the bladder. (Just to be clear: puncturing bladder or intestines is highly undesirable.) It is possible to start the incision under the chin as did Tristan, but that adds to the length of the seam and increases the likelihood that the body cavity will be exposed to contaminants such as dirt, grit, weeds, and hair. Best to dress a deer using the shortest seam possible.

Push your fingers into the incision to widen it and create a space between the smooth muscle and the soft guts. Feel free to poke the guts with your fingertips, but remember that a hernia is what happens when the peritoneal sac (the gut sack) tears, and the innards begin to bulge out. Carefully slide your gutting knife in between your fingers, cutting edge facing up, making very sure that the tip does not rip the peritoneal sac, and push the blade away from you while pressing in an upward motion. The idea is to make an incision that starts at the breastbone and extends to the genitals while taking care to avoid snagging the tip of the knife on any part of the guts. Once your knife arrives at the penis and testicles, cut them off with as little disturbance as possible, and continue the incision until you've reached the anus. Then stop.

Now that this long incision is complete, pull apart the seam with your hands, exposing the guts, and take a good whiff. They should smell like fresh blood and not like putrefaction, illness, or decay. The odor ought to be slightly salty and sharper than fresh red meat from the butcher. If the peritoneal sac is intact, puncture it carefully to expose the viscera directly. Assess the internal damage and determine the trajectory of the bullet or arrow in order to avoid cutting yourself on shattered ribs. A deer fatally shot anywhere in the torso will have a lot of internal bleeding, but the organs themselves ought to appear healthy. This is also the first opportunity to assess the future quality of the venison by looking for fat tucked around organs and lining the ribcage. From the cook's standpoint, yellow fat globules clinging to heart, liver, and kidneys, as well as thick rinds of fat on the ribs, are highly desirable.

There are two ways to free the guts from the lower end of the alimentary canal, otherwise known as the anus. Here is the first way: from the outside, make deep, 3-4 inch cuts all the way around the anus (the anus and the vulva, if female). Do not cut into the anus itself. Once that circular cut is complete, reach back in from the incision and tie the bowels off from the inside, getting as close as possible to the anal opening. The lower intestines may be full of deer pellets that feel like marbles. It's not gross, relatively speaking, and because the pellets haven't been exposed to oxygen, they won't smell unless the deer has been paunched. (If it has, your nose will know it.) Push the tied-off anus into the body cavity by knocking it loose from the outside. This step frees the lower end of the alimentary canal from the rest of the deer's body.

Here is the second way: With the deer still on its back and its hind legs splayed, split the pelvic bone with a good whack with a hunting knife or using a specialty item called a pelvic saw. Halved, the pelvic bone can be pulled apart, and the anus tied off and cut out from above rather than dug from outside. The second way is perhaps the better choice from the standpoint of preserving venison because it involves less disturbance around areas where scent glands are concentrated.

As soon as this step is accomplished, locate the bladder, pinch it off at the base of the urinary tract, and cut the urethra (pee tube). If you like, save the urine and use it for a scent drip. Ambitious sorts come prepared with an empty bottle to fill.

To loosen the remaining viscera from the body cavity, a few more cuts of internal membranes (called mesentery) will probably be necessary. This can generally be accomplished by tugging gently with your hands or a few judicious pokes with the knife. The guts should now be spilling out. It's a bit of a mess but the intestines should be pink, firm, and robust in appearance. Reach up and free the entire mass by cutting the esophageal tube above the stomach, roll the deer on its side, scoop the guts out with your hands, and then return the deer on its back. The guts should stay put on the ground.

Now is a good point to take stock of your surroundings. Remember that you are in the wild and the lush smell of fresh blood will attract carnivores that might be around. Deer hunters tells stories of field dressing their quarry, happily absorbed in their task, only to turn around and find themselves facing an interested bear—or, in the figure below, a wild boar.

WILD BOAR, SHEEP & BUTCHER

William Samuel Howitt, Wild boar threatens a flock, 1821. Credit: Wellcome Institute.

In the event there are no bears around, a few more steps will complete the job. To finish emptying out the body cavity, cut through the thin membrane called the diaphragm to get to the heart and liver. The liver should be dark red, flexible, and free of white spots. Pull out the liver and heart, put them aside, and save them for supper. Then roll up your sleeves, reach inside and up into the neck with your hand, grab the esophagus, trachea and windpipe, and yank down hard to release it from the upper end of the alimentary canal (the mouth) and also detach the lungs from the breathing apparatus called "the nose." If yanking doesn't work, use your knife to cut the windpipe etc., but be careful not to slice your fingers as this must be done by feel. It can also be undertaken by cutting from the outside, in the manner of performing a tracheotomy, but this approach ruins the head for taxidermy and is also messier in general.

As soon as the lungs are free, tip the deer on its side and let the remaining viscera roll out gently. Throw the lungs on the gut pile, and let the cavity drain. If urine, fecal matter, or scent from scent glands has contaminated your hands or the body cavity any time during this operation, rinse the cavity out quickly with snow or salt water (if available), then immediately blot up any excess moisture with paper towels or food-grade cloth rags. Do not reuse the rags. Do not pack the cavity with snow or ice.

Moisture inside the cavity encourages flies to land and bacteria to grow. Bacteria is not your friend. This is why so many old hunting manuals admonished hunters to simply wipe the body cavity with a clean cloth without using water. Correspondingly, earlier editions of the *The Joy of Cooking* (first published in 1931) advised dusting the body cavity with black pepper or powdered charcoal to absorb moisture, slow spoilage, and keep flies off it. (Salt cannot be used, as it will draw out too much moisture from the meat and end up partly curing it.) *The Joy of Cooking* did not recommend hosing it out. Once again, no water. To our eyes, a washed cavity looks neater and seems better. Cleaner. More hygienic, etc. But unless you're using distilled water—which is to say, sanitized water—you're throwing bacteria inside and giving them a perfect environment in which to proliferate.

Untreated water can carry microorganisms such as listeria, which enjoys cold temperatures and causes listeriosis (muscle aches, convulsions, and other unpleasant symptoms). It also contains pathogens from wildlife poo. It's for this reason that campers are warned not to drink from the lake even when they're thirsty, and to always boil the water if they're taking it from brooks, streams and snow. As far as washing carcasses is concerned, the tradition of dry-wiping it is less imperative today since potable tap water is readily available, flowing even through garden hoses. It's still a good idea to keep the interior of the carcass as dry as possible. In cold climates, adding water will damage the venison when that water turns to ice after dark. Hunters in warm climates often bring coolers full of ice on their hunts, figuring that the benefits of swift cooling outweigh the risks of spreading around fecal contaminants and bacteria thanks to melting ice water. Keep the carcass up off the ice itself by placing it on a shelf inside the cooler. Once that lid is shut, it's easy to forget that a deer resting up on bags of ice will soon turn into a deer bathing in bloody water full of interesting microorganisms.

Here are some of the bacteria found in deer intestines: *Clostridium perfringens*, *Listeria monocytogenes*, *Heliobacter pylori* (formerly *Campylobacter pylori*), *Yersinia enterocolitica*, *Francisella tularemia*, *Coxiella burnetii*, and *Salmonella*. A 2008 report by Cornell University's Waste Management Institute, in conjunction with various experts, identified these pathogens and assessed their prevalence in wild deer roadkill in New York State (*Pathogen Analysis of NYSDOT Road-Killed Deer Carcass Compost Facilities for Task Assignment C-04-01 PIN R020.63.881 Temperature and Pathogen Final Report*, September 17, 2008.) They found little evidence of Salmonella, Listeria, Campylobacter, and Coxiella. By contrast, E. coli, Yersina, Tularemia, Giardia, and Clostridium were present, this last being especially prevalent in the gut, and multiplying rapidly when the animal dies. If consumed by humans, these pathogens can cause serious illness. Though their study focused on roadkill whitetail in one East Coast state, the Cornell team's findings can be understood to broadly apply to whitetail in this country.

This information is not meant to be scary. Given that many of these same pathogens exist in livestock animals and, in some cases, are the reason why the whitetails have started carrying them thanks to fecal cross-contamination (grass-fed cattle and deer can graze the same farmland), the risks of contracting a food-borne illness from consuming wild venison are no greater and possibly less than consuming any factory-farmed food. Approximately 48 million Americans contract a food-borne illness every year. In 2013, a report released by the Center for Disease Control and Prevention analyzed the statistics on food-borne illnesses in the United States from 1998-2008, and discovered, somewhat to their surprise, that the largest vector was leafy greens (lettuce, spinach, and kale), which accounted for 23 percent of illnesses. Poultry was next, followed by dairy products—very specifically, raw milk. Combined with good field dressing techniques, the hunter's awareness that these pathogens exist will ensure that the venison is healthy in every sense of the word.

Thanks to YouTube, thousands of demonstration videos on the internet have helped demystify the process. Field dressing is as easy as it seems, and harder than it looks. Putting it bluntly: the deer is dead. You cannot hurt it. It doesn't feel pain. The most difficult part about the operation is wielding the knife like a scalpel, recognizing that it has to perform several different tasks such as incising, cutting, digging, and whacking. These actions reflect the varied textures of an interior body that is rarely confronted in everyday life. It's also being aware that the deer has guts. A lot of them. Those guts are still teeming with life forms capable of striking back if they're not treated with care and respect.

As with most things, field dressing takes practice. But what first-timers and curiosity seekers want to know is how it *feels*, and by this they not only mean the feel of the blade against skin, but how you feel about it. Grateful? Conflicted? Grossed out? None of the above? The answer lies in the thoughts running through your head. There will be blood on your hands, but that is the price for good venison on your table.

× DRAG: GETTING THE DEER OUT OF THE WOODS

The dressed deer has to be brought out, preferably in one piece, so it can be weighed, inspected, and registered at a deer inspection station. Today's hunters have the option of tying the deer on a motorized vehicle such as an ATV in fall and a Skidoo in winter, and driving it out of the bush, the forest, or the field where it fell. Some hunters try to hunt near remote roads so they can winch it into a nearby pickup truck. Some hunt near a river, where they can lie in wait for thirsty deer to come by, and have a boat waiting to carry away their quarry. But even if modern transport is available, some amount of dragging is required. Thus, hunters still need to know how to carry out a deer without benefit of a motorized vehicle, and be prepared with the necessary tools.

This portion of the hunt can come as a surpise. When hunting takes place in popular culture—movies, literature, and the like—it focuses on the fatal shot, then all of a sudden, it cuts to a scene of a bunch of guys standing around a campfire, roasting a haunch of venison on a spit. It's so common to leave out the intermediary parts that it doesn't even occur to people to wonder what happened.

To get the quarry out of the woods and into the frying pan, so to speak, is a matter of logistics but also sheer strength and stubbornness. The mechanics of moving a dead body niggle at the back of the head of anyone who has ever seen a photograph of a hunter posing with a two-ton moose, muskox, or similarly immense quarry. That's two thousand pounds of droopy weight. Surely they don't just leave it? But it's so heavy! Where's the forklift? There must be a story ... A scene in the Civil War film *Cold Mountain* revolves around a one-ton domestic cow that has expired in a brook. The decomposing body must be removed lest it contaminate the water supply, but the lonely farmer can't budge it. Along come a Confederate deserter and a defrocked preacher who just happen to be carrying a twelve-foot crosscut saw, and the cow ends up being sawn up "in chapters" back to front like an enormous bread loaf. They did not eat it for supper.

Because hunters cannot count on running into strangers who just happen to be carrying around the perfect tool for the task at hand, they must learn other techniques to carry large quarry out of the field. When the quarry proves to be more than two men can carry out using an improvised stretcher or something similar, field dressing extends to quartering the animal on the spot. Following Tristan's process, it will be chunked into portions—the head being one chunk, the haunches another, the shoulders yet another, and so on, with special rules depending on the animal and the region—and carried out in manageable portions by anyone who is around to help. The chunks end up being approximately the weight of a whitetail, anywhere from 90 to 250 pounds before it's dressed in the field.

It is not easy to walk around carrying 90 extra pounds, let alone 250, especially when it comes in an irregular shape and is covered in fur. The slipperiness of the deer's fur explains how it can move so easily through thick brush, but it also makes the body difficult to handle when you attempt to pick it up. The entire carcass will flop heavily in your hands. After you've prodded and poked it into the best position for it to be carried, it will tip over in a heap if rigor mortis hasn't set in. If rigor has set in, the deer will be as stiff and unbendable as a board, causing a whole new set of frustrations. The last thing the hunter wants is for the meat to be contaminated, but field dressing means there's a body cavity vulnerable to picking up dirt, grass, and insects. In short, carrying out a deer poses significant challenges, and while some of the tools have gotten fancier, the basics remain the same. It's still good to hunt in a group, or to be close enough to a hunting camp that you can walk back and get help. Help is very helpful.

This photograph documents two traditional methods of carrying out the quarry.

Anonymous, Return from the hunt, photo, c. 1922. Five hunters with hunting dogs, carrying two deer. Library of Congress.

Upside down, the whitetail buck is being carried by two men using a single pole balanced on their left shoulders. They've tied the buck's legs together and fastened them to a straight sapling cut down to serve this purpose. The problems with this method are immediately evident. The buck's head hangs low, and his antlers threaten to catch on every patch of tall grass. Walking will cause the buck to sway back and forth, creating a pendulum effect that will force the men to compensate in order to keep from losing their balance.

The better alternative is the two-pole method, which works by bundling the deer up, tucking its legs under, and fastening it head-up between two poles. No dangling, no swaying movement, no danger of the antlers catching on the ground, and better distribution of the carrying load as both shoulders are doing the supporting.

Both the one-pole and two-pole methods require two men, handy trees to cut down, a hatchet, and a length of rope. When trees are not available or the hunter has no help, another method is the "sling." This is the method being used by the hunter on the left side of the photograph on the previous page from 1922. He has hog-tied all four legs together, transforming the limbs into a makeshift strap. Carried close to the body, the doe becomes a furry purse. The limits of this method are also readily apparent. It only works when the deer is small and the hunter is strong enough to walk on uneven terrain while carrying a lopsided burden.

Another option for the solo hunter is the "knapsack" method, which involves draping the deer over your shoulders in the manner of a bony fur stole. Looking at these old photos, one has to wonder if deer hunters a century ago drank testosterone for breakfast, but this guy tops them by carrying his deer out on skis.

"Toting" the game—skeeing [sic] in the Bad Lands, Montana, c. 1902, stereograph. Hunter on skis carrying dead deer on his shoulders. Credit: International View Co.

To stabilize the load and solve the slippery problem of the deer's tendency to flop, he has fastened its legs to a makeshift pole. Based on the shape of its neck and its overall size, this whitetail is likely a doe, though it is possibly a winter buck with dropped antlers. Either way, it's astonishing that a man hunting in the Badlands of Montana managed to stand up on his wooden skis without poles, let alone slide across the snow with a deer slung around his neck. Given the effort that he's putting into this project, it's evident that this man is hunting for food and not for sport: despite the fact that he's on skis, he's not playing. He's determined to get the deer out because he needs the calories.

Less ambitious winter hunters just drag their deer out. Unglamorous as it may be, this is pretty much how it's still done.

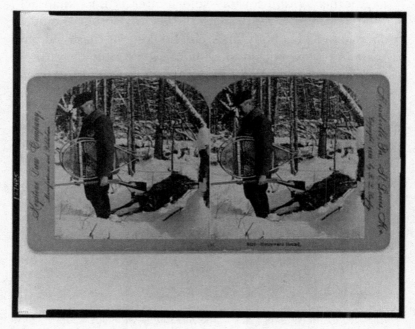

"Homeward Bound," Hunter, holding a rifle and snowshoes under arm, drags slain deer through the snow, stereograph, 1899. Credit: Keystone View Co.

Taken in 1899, this photograph shows a man who's been hunting in deep powder snow, as evidenced by the amount of float provided by his snowshoes. He's tied a length of a standard cotton rope around the doe's neck, then used that same piece of rope to run a half hitch around the snout. Then he grabbed the other end, wrapped it around his bare hand, and dragged it one-handed behind him. When there's no snow, some hunters wrap the deer in a canvas tarp, improvise a stretcher out of sapling poles, or use a new-fangled metal deer cart with wheels. Alternately, if the deer is a buck and the terrain is mostly soft grass, the easiest thing is to just grab him by the horns and drag.

"Easiest" is not easy, but there's no way to skip it. The best way to get the quarry out depends on the specific configuration of the terrain being hunted and the number of hunters available to help. It is at this moment that the hunt pivots away from skills and stamina, and to the sheer upper body strength required for lifting, dragging, and carrying a hundred pounds or more down a nonexistent trail. Many women gravitate toward hunting small game for this reason, which is not the same as saying that women cannot carry out large game. Miki Collins and her sister both live in Alaska, hunt moose, and bring it out by themselves, noting that a "come along" (a ratchet lever winch) is a very helpful tool. But the reality is that carrying a large cervid out poses a real physical challenge for many men and most women that no amount of political correctness can change.

Here is where old myths must be engaged.

Specifically, it's still the case that current ideas about hunting tap into vague but persistent notions regarding traditions held by Native Americans. In the photograph on page 78, for example, a very young boy is carrying out a deer that is considerably larger than him. (For inexplicable reasons, the deer is missing its forelegs.) Though there is certainly no dearth of records that confirm the fact that Native Americans hunted deer for food, what this image actually represents is a 1908 reenactment of "The Song of Hiawatha," 1855, the

No 10   Hiawatha.

Reenactment of "Song of Hiawatha" by Henry Wadsworth Longfellow, showing boy, "Hiawatha," dragging deer, 1908, Library of Congress.

epic poem by American poet Henry Wadsworth Longfellow, which remains one of the most influential and widely read works of American poetry ever written.

One of the poem's most familiar portions describes Hiawatha on a deer hunt. He is hidden in the bushes, waiting patiently for a deer to show up. Finally, he is excited to see a roebuck coming down the path. He raises his bow and places his arrow, making ready to aim, but the small motion startles the "roebuck," which leaps into the air—too late to avoid the fatal arrow. It drops dead with one shot. Triumphantly, Hiawatha carries his "red deer" out of the glowing woods and back to his tribe, where he makes a cloak from its hide and holds a feast so his entire tribe can enjoy the venison.

This is a Romantic vision of the lives of Native Americans, and literary critics have routinely pointed out that Longfellow made up the information. For example, Longfellow calls the quarry a "roebuck." Then he calls it a "red deer." The roe deer is reddish in color, but Longfellow doesn't seem to be aware that there was a separate species called the red deer, and they were not interchangeable. More to the point, neither roe deer nor red deer have ever been present in the Midwest, so Hiawatha could not have been hunting them. It's as odd as having him hunt giraffes. However, roe deer and red deer *are* still plentiful in England, and Longfellow was often accused of imitating the Romantic poets who lived there.

Just as the "roe/red deer" bit is made up, so too is the fiction of Native Americans hunting with a simple recurve bow and dropping a mature buck with one shot, especially if the hunter pulling the bowstring back was a five-year-old boy using a bow sized for children. What is true is that this odd image conveys how it feels to carry out a deer on foot: dwarfed by the enormity of the task, staggering under the burden, tired myths evaporating with every step and the realization that there's miles to go ahead. It's just hard, slogging work, with dirty hands and your face up a deer's butt.

× SKINNING TEETH

The next step is hanging, a process that can save the venison of a deer that's old and stressed, and make it tender and even superb. For this reason, the need to separate out fact from fiction becomes more urgent, because getting confused can mean the difference between a delicious supper or a terrible meal.

The fictions abound. Here is one example: "Ree Dolly stood at break of day on her cold front steps and smelled coming flurries and saw meat. Meat hung from trees across the street. The carcasses hung pale of flesh with a fatty gleam from low limbs of saplings in the side yards." This was venison, writes Daniel Woodrell, author of *Winter's Bone*, "venison left to the weather for two nights and three days so the early blossoming of decay might round the flavor, sweeten that meat to the bone."

Man with shotgun at doorway of cabin and a deer hanging from pole at camp, Eighth Lake, Fulton Chain, Adirondack Mountains, N.Y., 1892. Library of Congress.

In this case, we're talking about actual fiction—Southern Gothic writing, to be exact. It's true that many people who grew up in both North and South are familiar with the sight of gutted deer hanging off trees. It's also true that Woodrell's a novelist. He's not going for documentary description. But the inaccuracies here are useful because they're a good reflection of the errors floating around in contemporary culture.

Some of them have to do with terms. Some of them have to do with practice. While the corrections may seem minor, they matter if you're trying to turn a deer into venison.

1. Just as a living deer isn't a walking carcass, a hanging deer is not yet venison.
2. Hanging doesn't affect the flavor of the meat directly. It affects its texture and moisture content, which the brain lumps together with flavor and interprets as "taste."
3. Decay doesn't "sweeten" the meat. Decay is decay.
4. Nobody leaves an exposed, skinned carcass out to swing from a tree, especially when the temperatures are above freezing. Doing so invites flies to lay their eggs, birds to poo, scavengers to snack, and carnivores to steal the entire thing.
5. If the carcass is being hung in order to tenderize the meat, two days and three nights isn't long enough to achieve the desired results.

Whether or not the Dollys of Appalachia would have skinned the deer before they hung it is debatable, but it's important to clarify why a deer would be hanging from a tree in the first place. Immediately after gutting, hunters hang up their deer so it can be cooled and fully drained. This decision is related to the mechanical practicalities of exposing as much surface as possible to air in order to prevent bacteria from growing. When the outdoor temperatures are around freezing, cooling will more or less happen by dint of the weather. In warmer climates, however, spoilage begins the moment the deer goes down. The faster cooling begins, the more likely the venison will be preserved in best possible condition.

This operation is not the same as "hanging a deer." To hang a deer refers to a decision to leave the cooled and drained carcass suspended in regulated temperatures between 33°F and 38°F degrees for at least 11 days and no more than two weeks. During this time, the meat ages. However, the process is stopped before it becomes "aged meat." (More on this in the next chapter.)

It's partly because people are talking about different things that they have such wildly contrasting views on the subject of hanging. Sometimes a deer is skinned prior to being hung. Sometimes it's not. Some people think that hanging makes no difference. Sometimes they're right. There are two main schools of thought on the subject of hanging/skinning, and it's a bit like politics: the two sides will never agree on the best way to proceed. Like everything regarding the quarry, it is to be determined on a case-by-case basis. Because every hunt is different, each set of circumstances is unique. However, the variables are finite. Assuming that the hunt was clean and the kill was swift, the following generalities apply:

- If the deer is a young buck (spikehorn or forkhorn) or young doe and has been gutted out *before* rigor has set in, hanging will do little to improve it. Proceed with skinning and butchering.
- If the deer is a young buck or doe and reached rigor, dress and hang the deer in a cold (38°F degrees) environment until the muscles relax, about 24 hours and up to three days, then proceed with skinning and butchering.
- If the deer is a medium-weight buck or doe and has been dressed before rigor has set in, hanging for up to eleven days in a cold-controlled environment will tenderize it. If a buck, skin before hanging.
- If the deer is a large mature buck, hanging is imperative, up to two weeks in a cold, temperature-controlled environment. Skin before hanging.

In any instances where the deer was pushed or stressed, extended hanging will tenderize the venison though it will not improve the taste. This is why the default is to hang for 11 to 14 days, so as to remove the guesswork from this stage.

In this typical hunting camp photo from 1907, two men in shirtsleeves have hung up bucks and are preparing to work on them.

"Skinning the deer," c. 1907, Library of Congress.

A few details are worth noting: there is no snow on the ground, the woolen shirts worn by the men are enough to keep them warm, the bucks are both large and mature, and neither was field dressed before being hung. Indeed, only the Badlands skier was carrying a deer that had been dressed in the field, showing that the conventional wisdom does slowly change even in an activity as tradition-bound as hunting.

Despite the fact that this scene looks like every other old hunting camp photo you've ever seen, with men waiting around for wet gear to dry as they get ready to throw a haunch of venison on the campfire, the details reveal significant differences from today's hunting camps, and it's not just because today's campers now wear camouflage, use scopes on their rifles, and pitch pop-ups made of nylon. At first glance, it may look like these hunters were skinning their deer. But what they were actually doing was bleeding and gutting the quarry. More importantly, their rationale for proceeding in this particular fashion, was totally unrelated to the reasons held today.

As discussed previously, medical science (and military surgery in particular) emphasized the importance of swift and competent field dressing. The intestines teem with bacteria. For a living organism, these bacteria are largely beneficial, but as soon as the heart and lungs stop working, they start overpopulating their newly oxygen-free environment. (Fun fact: there are ten times more bacteria in the human body than there are human cells.) The faster the intestines exit the body, the higher the chances the meat will remain "fresh"—this being a specific term indicating that it hasn't started decomposition.

Quick evacuation of the intestines explains why a deer can hang for several weeks without spoiling. If the body was initially cooled very rapidly, and then kept consistently at refrigeration temperatures, the meat will be firm and "fresh" after two weeks. Hanging is not about introducing decay. Rather, it's entirely focused on preventing it.

At the opening of the 20th century, hunters did not have this information. Instead of hanging the deer in order to dry, cool, and relax the body following rigor mortis, they believed that hanging helped drain the blood. In this respect, they were borrowing slaughtering/butchering conventions used for pigs. Thus, in 1916, G. B. Buchanan recommended that hunters "bleed" their deer as soon as it was down, and for this purpose it should be hung up by its hind legs. If the deer was going to be hanging in bad weather, however, "it should be turned around and hung head up," Buchanan recommended, as this method encouraged rainwater and snow to travel in the direction of the hairs. (Again, "hung" in this context merely refers to the physical state of suspension, not to the processing "being hung" in order to tenderize the meat.) He also added that the entrails "ought to be removed," preferably before carrying the buck back to camp, but this step came after the deer had been strung up to keep it off the ground, and often did not happen until the next day, or whenever it could be retrieved. The fact that the guts were left in indefinitely explains why he believed that "fresh killed venison" was too strong "for some palates," and thus the meat was best after having "ripened a bit."

Livestock pigs are still stuck, hung, and bled, and it all happens very quickly before it moves on to gutting.

John Collier, Ephrata, Pennsylvania (vicinity). Butchering pork on a Mennonite farm, 1942, showing a pig that has been stuck, hung, bled, and in the process of being gutted.

Formerly, then, deer and pigs underwent identical steps in the same sequence. So:

Pig: stuck, hung, bled, gutted.

Deer: shot, hung, bled, gutted.

Regarding wild deer taken in the hunt, it is now understood that sticking and bleeding are unnecessary steps, because the shot exsanguinates the quarry. However, as a result of the "sticking and bleeding" theory, which persisted in hunting literature well into the 1950s, the deer's entrails were often left in too long and the venison inevitably started to decompose in the warm weather. This was not good for anyone. It's still not good, which is why field dressing is now a priority. Today, the sequence is:

Deer: shot (bled), gutted, hung.

The reasons for and against skinning before hanging, however, are not so direct, and are a combination of factors related to ambient conditions; whether or not the deer is old and male; if you plan on skinning the deer yourself, and whether you will have help. It is significantly easier to skin a deer while the body is still warm and the hide is loose. This is especially true in cold weather, for a frozen hide won't bend. There are now purpose-built gambrels, or a triangle with hooks that anchors the hindquarters in position. These hooks slide into notches the hunter punches between the tendon and the bone of the hind leg just before the hoof. Gambrels often come with pulleys to help hoist the quarry up: the deer must be securely hung from a reliably strong beam or else it will crash down on your head during skinning.

The cuts start with circular incisions all around the hind leg at the point closest to the hooves, then incising down the inside of the back legs toward the pelvis. Repeat on the other side. Then peel the skin, starting from the heels, and yank down with as much force as necessary. The skin on the back legs will cling, but once you are beyond the pelvis and have cut off the tail bone, it will pull away in great sheets starting with the rump. Keep peeling and tugging until you reach the head. Using a clean and disinfected bone saw, saw the head off, followed by the front legs at the knees. Then tug. The hide should now be off. During this process, be aware that the hide is thicker and heavier than it looks and the little hairs get everywhere, so the fewer cuts, the better. Hair that gets on the meat will not wash off easily.

The technique lies mostly in the swiping motion that goes through subcutaneous fat while avoiding slicing through muscle on one side and hide on the other. Use hands and fingers as much as possible; the fat layer will yield, especially when the body is still warm. A skinning knife assists in places where the subcutaneous layer is tightly bound to the skin, chiefly around the back legs, the pelvis, and the shoulders.

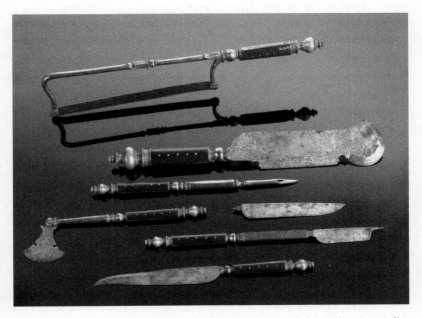

"The hunting trousse contains all the instruments needed by a hunter to dismember and prepare a deer. It includes a needle, saws, and knives with different shaped blades, including a skinning knife. They are ornately decorated with brass and the steel blades are engraved. These instruments could also be used for surgery. The same craftsman who made this set might also have made surgical instruments." Science Museum, London.

This is a short-bladed knife with a rounded edge that allows scraping as well as cutting, and helps prevent accidental poking that is too easy with a conventional blade's sharp tip. Good technique will save the hide for future use, but the deer doesn't care if you accidentally slice off muscle or poke a few holes in it.

If the deer is a doe, it can be hung without being skinned. If venison is a priority, however, an old buck should be skinned because the oils in the hair and the scent from its glands will transfer to the venison, infusing it with unpleasant flavors. Advocates of hanging the deer in its hide will complain that the exposed flesh will dry out and darken as it forms an inedible rind. This is true, but it is better to lose an inch than to risk tainting the entire carcass. Removal of the hide also speeds the cooling of larger animals, which is why beef carcasses are always skinned before hanging under temperature- and moisture-controlled conditions.

Remove the tenderloins, which are two strips of muscle inside the body cavity, running down both sides of the spine. In beef, this cut becomes filet mignon. It is so delicate that it is usually possible to just pull it out after freeing the muscle at the top with a small starting cut to avoid tearing it. Set it aside with the liver and the heart, which should be already in the refrigerator.

All modern manuals recommend hanging the carcass head down because it discourages blood from pooling in the haunches and infusing these choice cuts of meat with a fishy flavor. The head-down position also speeds cooling because the legs are propped apart. Encouraging the blood to flow toward the head is a simple way to instantly improve the quality of the venison, as the hindquarters, tenderloins, and back straps are now considered the most valuable cuts, and the head and neck the least desirable. It should be noted that these priorities are not obvious; by the 15th century, the most valued cuts were the head and neck, and the legs were given

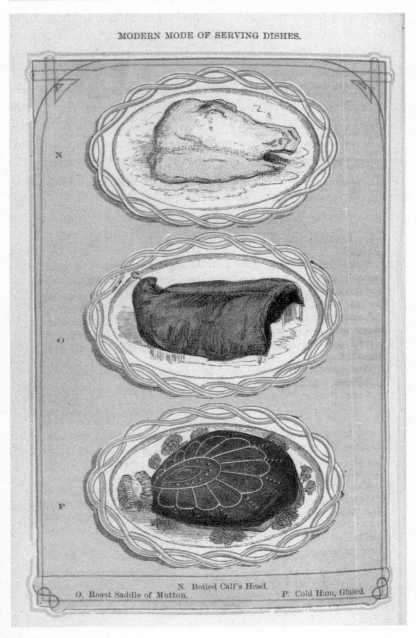

MODERN MODE OF SERVING DISHES.

N. Boiled Calf's Head.
O. Roast Saddle of Mutton.
P. Cold Ham, Glazed.

Credit: Wellcome Institute.

to people of lower rank. The hierarchy began to shift in the mid-19th century, as seen in the illustration on the previous page to *Mrs. Beeton's Book of Household Management*, which presents a mixed compilation of N) Boiled calf's head, O) Boiled saddle of mutton, and P) Cold ham, glazed, 1861. Though all these portions are desirable, it's the high levels of fat itself that unites them, not the cuts per se or their points of origin on the body

Head down and hands folded, the hunter is now a penitent as well as a provider. Now begins the waiting: as the hanging deer becomes a deer being hung, it's a carcass in the shed, not meat on the table. Bait for wolves, not food for people. Hanging in suspended animation, the deer carcass is still not yet venison. But the most prized bits—the liver, heart, and tenderloins—should be consumed immediately. Delicacies, they cannot be bought but have already been paid for. This is the essence of wild eating.

CHAPTER FOUR
Getting To the Meat of It

× LEFT HANGING

The skinned body is now a carcass. Exsanguination, or loss of blood, means that the body had been floppy. No blood pressure, because all the blood ran out. The question is: should the carcass be left to hang for a few days, or should it be butchered right away? Medieval history and modern food science provide some answers. One of the important variables is rigor mortis.

Rigor mortis is the stiffening of the body that occurs anywhere from four to six hours after death. What causes this sudden stiffening? Does it impact the quality of venison? It begins when mammals stop breathing, and cells are no longer supplied with oxygen. Lack of oxygen not only means that populations of bacteria will suddenly be exploding inside the guts, but that the fifty trillion cells that make up 130 pounds of your average mammal will no longer be able to respire.

This results in the incomplete diffusion of calcium ions from high to low areas of concentration. The muscles contract and stiffen, affecting every muscle in the body from the eyelids to the heart. Usually within 24 hours, enzymatic and bacterial activity break the muscle tissue down. This causes the muscles to relax but it is also the first sign of decomposition.

There is very little specific research on processing wild deer for human consumption, but a great deal of laboratory investigation regarding the best way to make cattle tender, tasty and appealing to consumers. These questions regarding rigor mortis, hanging, and cold storage are extremely important to the profit margins of the meat industry and consequently to food scientists, who conduct fascinating experiments and publish their findings in academic journals with names such as *Studies in Meat Tenderness*. Here is what they discovered by experimenting on livestock sheep and cows: To their great surprise, it turns out that if the carcass is butchered *before* rigor mortis has set in, the meat will be just as tender as meat carved off carcasses that had been conditioned by at least 48 hours of controlled-temperature hanging.

Aha! Suddenly, it makes sense that hunters who live in deer-crowded areas tend to advocate for the no-hanging-required approach. "Deer-crowded areas" often means there's a nearby cornfield or apple orchard attracting a herd, which also suggests calm, fat deer dropped quietly as they munched on crisp fruit. Lactic acid produced by exertion speeds up the onset of rigor, as does the increased muscle mass that comes with being a male. These two factors means that a muscular, combative quarry will reach rigor more quickly, and stay longer in that state, than a foolish pudgy youngster that never saw the hunter coming. Mature bucks that have been hunted hard are also far more likely to run off after being fatally shot, eluding immediate discovery. In which case, after the buck has been found, field dressed, and carried out, hanging must take place in order for the meat to be tender enough for humans to choke it down.

Interestingly, food scientists have also discovered that chilling the meat very quickly after slaughter produces undesirable effects. It makes the meat tough. This toughness is a consequence of "cold shortening." A descriptive and scientific term, "cold shortening" refers to the effect of cold temperatures on the basic unit of the muscle called sarcomeres, otherwise known as "fibers." Cold temperatures make the fibers contract, reducing their original length by up to a third, and they don't relax again, making the meat chewy and tough. The scientists were even more surprised to discover that hanging the carcass under controlled refrigerated conditions did not substantially improve the toughness. Once the fibers contracted, in other words, they stayed contracted, no matter how carefully it was cooked. (The "toughness" was tested the old-fashioned way: by chewing.)

In cold shortening, the basic mechanism is triggered by near-freezing temperatures combined with high pH levels associated with the conversion of glycolic acid to lactic acid due to anaerobic conditions in the muscles. In other words, it happens when the carcass is chilled too close to rigor. The body temperature of a mature whitetail is 104°F degrees, which is about one degree higher than a standard beef cow. Thus, much the same considerations apply regarding the risk of cold shortening. The chill temperature that produced the cold-shortening effect on beef was 34.6°F (2°C), which is a fairly dramatic drop to achieve. Most home butchers do not have freezer facilities that can chill a deer carcass that quickly. But this information regarding the cold-shortening effect is especially useful for hunters active in winter or in a cold climate where ambient temperatures can be expected to fall below freezing in the evening. Typically the worry is to prevent the carcass from freezing, not to prevent cold shortening. Both freezing and cold shortening damage the meat, but in different ways: freezing will make the meat mushy, whereas cold shortening will make it tough. Once either event occurs, there is no way to repair the cellular damage.

Beef carcasses on the production line, packing plant, Austin, Texas, 1941.

The best approach thus prevents these two events from happening in the first place. Slow chilling of the beef carcass at 50°F (10°C), followed by regular hanging at refrigeration temperatures of 33-38°F degrees, did not produce the cold shortening effect. Both large bucks and beef carcasses are typically hung for between ten days to two weeks, which is a costly investment of time and money (refrigeration isn't free), and a long time for hungry hunters to wait. A balance must be found between the need to cool the carcass as quickly as possible to avoid decomposition, and the time required for slow chilling followed by hanging to avoid toughening the meat. If there is snow on the ground, slow chilling of the deer carcass is often achieved by default. The trick is to hang the deer for the time required to tenderize the venison, and to do so at refrigeration temperatures for up to two weeks to tenderize a large buck.

"Hanging" can take place inside the actual refrigerator, if there's room for cut-up pieces to fit in. This helps make it clear that a deer carcass being hung under controlled temperatures is not "rotting." Rotting is a function of microbial activity. By contrast, the time allotted for hanging allows enzymes to break down collagen in the muscle tissue. If temperatures are too warm, dormant microbes and pathogens will wake up, causing spoilage. The standard refrigeration temperature range of 33-38°F slows decomposition while also ensuring that enzymes can still accomplish their task.

John Collier, Cured meat should be kept in a cool place, free from insects, mice, and rats, January 1942. Library of Congress.

All commercial beef carcasses are hung for around eleven days, which means that they are technically older at the end of the process than when they started. However, very few carcasses are "aged," which refers to a specific decision to extend the hanging beyond the initial 10-14 days, and to let it remain in suspension for another 14 to 35 days, and beyond. The traditional method is called dry-aging, which lets dry air do the work, just as it does in the initial hang time allotted to livestock carcasses.

According to food scientist Jeff W. Savell, the four main considerations regarding ensuring consistent results for aged beef are length of time, storage temperature, humidity, and air flow but, as he also points out, dry aging "may be more art than science."

Dry-aging—or just plain "aging"—is what makes ordinary ham into prosciutto by submitting a pig's haunch to up to two years of curing, but it's the "art" of the process that can turn it into *prosciutto di Parma*, Parma ham, using a method of preserving meat developed long before the invention of refrigeration. One of the world's great delicacies, this prosciutto can only be made in Parma, Italy, because it's as much a function of the particular qualities of this region's air as it is the artisanal secrets of its making.

Why should a deer hunter care about the methods used to create prosciutto and aged beef? Well, it's because some people claim that venison can't be aged, while others insist that it can. However, when hunters refer to "aging" their deer, they are usually thinking about *hanging* the deer, which allows the meat to get older by a few days but no longer than two weeks. Whereas the process of aging that leads to prosciutto and aged beef requires months and even years to complete.

By contrast, even a few weeks of extra hang time beyond the two-week mark for a haunch of venison is a good way to lose meat. It has to do with the fat content. Pork is fatty. The kind of beef selected for aging comes from Angus cows, which are bred to be heavily marbled with fat. When hams and beef are aged, they come out with a hardened rind and a buttery center because they start out tender and mildly flavored. By contrast, wild venison is finely grained and has almost no marbling. As J. Kenji Lopez-Alt informs me: "Aging wild meat is difficult because it tends to lack sufficient fat." (He is Chief Creative Officer of the food website SeriousEats.com) Venison also has a lower water content, making it a poor candidate for a long, slow, drying process that reduces the weight of the meat by over 30 percent through water evaporation. This evaporation concentrates the flavors of pork and beef, but venison already starts out more intensely flavored because it has less water than commercially raised livestock.

This is not to say that venison cannot be aged, because it can. But it's tricky precisely because wild game is unpredictable. It's entirely possible to spend a month aging a haunch of venison, only to discover that it started out gamy and ended up gamier. It's useful to note that no culture has developed a tradition of curing venison (or, for that matter, any wild meat except boar) by any form of extended, controlled, hanging. Smoking, yes, Pickling, yes. Baking and potting, yes. Aging, no. In this case, the absence of a tradition is revealing in itself.

× **THE CUT**

After the carcass finished its allotted time in the cooler, it should still be smelling fresh and feel springy and firm. Now, the hunter becomes a butcher. In Europe and the United Kingdom prior to industrialization, this position used to be dominated by powerful guilds, and the butcher held a social rank not unlike today's celebrity chefs: a safe but not-quite-civilized wielder of lethal tools inside the city, who earned large sums practicing a trade unfit for proper gentlemen.

Draped in a cow's hide and waving a leg of veal, the butcher on the next page is standing next to a table laden with blood sausages, kidneys, and lard. Holding up a plate of a head of veal proudly before her, the female butcher carries a whole suckling

A butcher; and a lady butcher. Credits: Wellcome Institute.

pig with an entire baby lamb flung over her shoulder. From head to tail, the entirety of these young animals was served at table, just as the brains, blood, and marrow were choice morsels from mature cows and pigs. Today, with the threat of chronic wasting disease (CWD), it is no longer recommended to consume these parts of any animal, whether domesticated or wild. For the home butcher, this means taking special care when splitting or quartering the carcass.

It used to be commonplace to recommend sawing exactly down the middle of the spine, exposing the length of the spinal cord to split the carcass into two halves called "sides." Hence a side of beef, or a side of buck, was literally one side of the animal. This method is no longer standard. Hunters doing their own butchering should first check with their state's Department of Game and Fishing to determine the risk of CWD, and only proceed when there's no evidence in the local deer population. CWD is a prion disease that attacks proteins in the brain and nervous system. It is always fatal in animals and humans. Given the outcome, I'd rather be overcautious and avoid that risk altogether since the consequences are so terrible. A spoiled bit of venison only causes a stomachache. Chronic wasting disease is deadly.

The only known natural hosts for CWD are deer (*Odocoileus* species, which includes mule deer and whitetail) and Rocky Mountain elk (*Cervus elaphus nelsoni*). It has also been found on deer farms, but the exact vectors remain unknown. Fatal cases in humans have been recorded in areas of the United States with known incidences of CWD in the wild deer and elk population, yet it is also the case that the overall rates of infection in wild animals is very low, and the rate of infection even lower in humans: about one in a million. What is also known, however, is that prion diseases have long incubation periods, and that animals can be visibly suffering for up to a year, which is a long time to be walking around with a poorly understood illness. For this reason, epidemiologists who have studied the question of deer-human transmission recommend that

> hunters should avoid eating meat from deer and elk that look sick or test positive for CWD. They should wear gloves when field-dressing carcasses, bone-out the meat from the animal, and minimize handling of brain and spinal cord tissues. As a precaution, hunters should avoid eating deer and elk tissues known to harbor the CWD agent (e.g., brain, spinal cord, eyes, spleen, tonsils, lymph nodes) from areas where CWD has been identified (*Journal of Infectious Diseases*, 2004).

"Boning-out" the meat means proceeding without cutting down the spine or any areas that might leak cerebrospinal fluid. The risk of CWD has also helped the premium cut called "the saddle" to fall out of fashion.

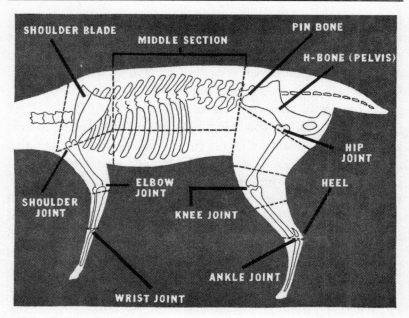

Butchering chart, large cuts.

If one imagines riding a deer, the "saddle" would be where the saddle would go. In butchery, the "saddle" starts after the last rib and ends at the last vertebra before hitting the pelvic bone, and includes the back straps on top and the tenderloins underneath, both still attached to the spine running down the center. The saddle is a decadent cut, a filet mignon crossed with rack of lamb, but the central presence of the spine means it's no longer popular. It its place: the new convention of taking the tenderloins and backstraps separately, and turning them into "medallions."

What this shift in safety means in practical terms is cutting off the legs and leaving the torso in one piece. In smaller deer (90 to 135 pounds), this is already an easier way to proceed because halving it is hardly worth the trouble. The butcher in the picture on page 98 holds a cleaver and carries a boning knife; a butcher's knife and a bone saw are also tools to have clean and ready before starting.

The delicate tenderloins should already have been taken out before hanging. Begin by taking the backstraps, which are thick skeins of meat running down the outside of the entire length of the spine. Starting at the top of the skein, which will be near the small of the rump, make a few judicious jabs with a short-bladed knife to dig them out and peel them down. Next, free the front legs by making a cut between the shoulder blades and the ribs. Pull the leg away from the body and take a good whack with the cleaver to separate the ball joint. Repeat on the other side. Take the carcass down, set it on a heavy worktable, and proceed to remove the back legs by separating the pelvic bone, digging until you find the hip joint, then cutting through by using the saw or the cleaver. Repeat on the other side.

Cut away the flanks from the lower belly (on a small deer, this meat will be thin and destined for grinding), and cut away the neck meat. Should you wish to save the ribs, take a saw and cut them off the spine. However, it's often the case that the ribs are shattered by the shot, in which case, at least one side will be too damaged to bother with after the damaged parts are cut out.

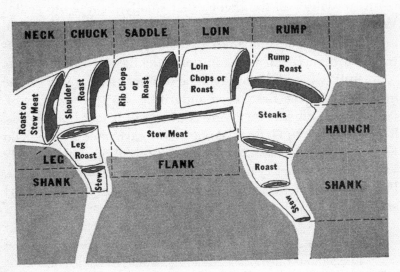

Butchering chart, small cuts.

This completes the large cuts. At this point, following the chart, the legs, rump, and haunches are further broken down into small, familiar cuts: steak, roasts, shanks, and so on, following the joints as well as the particularities of muscle groups.

Each cut should be identified and labeled with the following information before going into the freezer: sex (buck or doe), cut (shoulder, shank, etc.), the tag number, and freezing date.

× TO THE RESCUE

An ideal quarry, correctly dressed and hung, will yield tender and tasty venison with a distinctively rich but pleasant flavor. If any one of these previous steps encountered a glitch, the chef must rescue the venison by using tricks.

One of the oldest recorded tricks used to "recover [venison] when tainted," comes from Hannah Wooley's *Gentlewoman's Companion,* 1673: "Take a clean cloth and wrap your Venison therin, then bury it in the Earth one whole night, and it will take away the ill scent or favour." I confess that I haven't tried this because there hasn't been a need, but it seems to works on the theory that smelly meat is too acidic. Wherefore, if the soil is alkaline, it will absorb the odor in the manner of an enormous box of baking soda. This may neutralize the smell, but won't improve the flavor or the texture.

Still, what's most notable about her trick was that she included it in the first place, indicating that the tragedy of tainted venison was relatively common in better households. This reference to Hannah Wooley was excavated by The Old Foodie, Janet Clarkson, who shared a revealing entry of July 1660 from Samuel Pepys's diary. A member of Parliament, Pepys was Chief Secretary to the Admiralty under Charles II and later James II. He wrote:

I dined at my house in Seething lane. Thence to my Lord about business; and being in talk, in comes one

with half a Bucke from Hinchingbrooke, and it
smelling a little strong, my Lord did give it to me,
though it was as good as any could be. I did carry it
to my mother to dispose of as she pleased.

His mother decided to dispose of this strong-smelling side of
buck by baking it into a venison pasty. It being as "good as any
[venison] can be," she served the pasty to Pepys's wife and several guests two days later. Clearly, gamy venison that was already "high" or starting to spoil was still a respectable meal. In
August 1667, Pepys complained about dining at the home of Sir
W. Pen and being served "a damned venison pasty that stunk a
devil," further complaining that the meager table provided only
this smelly dish plus "a leg of mutton and a pullet or two."

What is a pasty? The Cornish pasty is a variation that has
survived today, but it's not a pastry, and it's not a pie. It is a stur-
dy crust baked around a filling, generally meat. In the case of
the Cornish pasty, the meat is beef. Though they could be small
enough to fit in the hand, they could also be very large, en-
compassing an entire side of venison buck, and thus could take
all day to roast. These pasties were a combination of baking
method and preserving, as keeping the meat in an age before
refrigeration was a constant challenge. Notably, there was no attempt to cure game in the manner of ham. Instead, as Clarkson
helpfully adds, another cookbook by Hannah Wooley, *The Cook's
Guide*, 1664, provides an interesting set of instructions to keep
"Venison nine or ten months good and sweet."

Take a haunch of Venison and bore holes in it, then
stop in seasoning into it as you do parsley into beef
in the inside of it if it be red Deer, take pepper, nutmeg, cloves, mace and salt; if it be fallow deer then
only pepper and salt; when it is thus seasoned dip it
in white wine vinegar, and put it in an earthen pot
with the salt side down and having first sprinkled

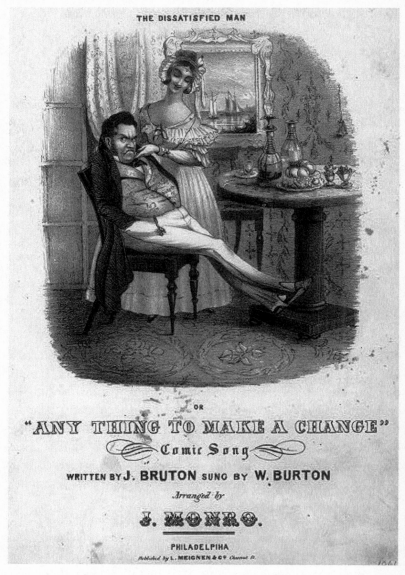

The Dissatisfied Man, or "Any Thing to Make a Change" [between 1830 and 1910], Library of Congress.

good store of spice into the pot; if it be fallow deer three pound of butter will serve, but if red deer then four pounds; when you put it into the oven lay an earthen dish over it, and paste it close up that no air can get out nor in, so let it stand six or seven hours in a very hot oven; when it is baked take off the cover and put in a trencher and a stone upon it to keep the meat down in the liquor; fill up the pot with melted butter and so keep it, serve it to the table in slices with mustard and sugar.

These directions are for red deer and fallow deer—which are notably not cooked in an identical fashion—but they would be applicable to whitetail deer if American diners today would be willing to consume a slice taken off a spiced and buttered haunch of venison that had been in an unrefrigerated earthen pot for ten months. My guess is the answer is no, because sensibilities have changed. Whereas in 17th-century Europe and England, the high culinary status of venison trumped the "damned stink" of it. No matter how strong or smelly, the venison would be eaten by those fortunate enough in the 17th century to get their hands on it, and these fortunate were not commoners – shopkeepers, business owners, and the like. They were lords, ladies, and members or the landed gentry.

Today, however, everyday Americans and Britons eat venison they hunt themselves, and most would prefer to avoid having to hold their nose as they dine. Below, I have listed some common problems, the explanations for why they happen, and their solutions.

It tastes gamy.
The taste called "gamy" is not a consequence of overcooking. It is also not in the fat. It is in the muscle tissue itself.

The taste called "gamy" is a strong, unappealing-to-inedible taste, distinct from the regular flavor profile of wild venison. It typically shows up in mature trophy bucks that have been hunted hard, leaving both hunter and quarry exhausted. As a result of prolonged running, the muscles will build up lactic acid and suffer micro-tears from exertion. (Muscles pushed past their usual limits provokes the feeling of "burn." The repairing of the micro-tears causes "bulking up.") The taste buds can detect this damage, and reject it as unpleasant. Combined with the more intense flavor profile of wild meat, the buildup of lactic acid, micro-damage, and other enzymatic activity connected to the adrenaline surge results in the taste called "gamy."

Notably, "gamy" tastes can occur in any animal, including domesticated livestock, which is one of the reasons why cattle are kept as still and calm as possible before slaughter. All wild game does a lot more running around than domesticated livestock, but larger whitetail and especially bucks (130 to 300 pounds) are more likely to be gamy because they are more difficult than a small doe or buck (90 to 130 pounds) to drop in a single shot. If they have been running around and then kept running after being shot, the venison will be gamy.

Solution: Go for the smaller, younger quarry, and be sure to drop it while it is standing quietly.

It smells funny.

Buck venison can also taste gamy if the "must" or "musk" from their scent glands gets onto the meat. If it does, the flavor will be off.

Mature bucks are particularly susceptible to being tainted in this fashion, because that scent can get all over their pelt, and thus difficult to avoid during field dressing. In an attempt to position the buck and keep it in place, you will rub up against the pelt, it will smear you with scent, and it will get into weird places. Wiping it off quickly can keep the scent from penetrating the meat, but there's still the problem of the scent that's all over your hands, clothes, and gear. It's another reason to stick to does and young bucks if hunting for venison.

Venison that smells funny will taste funny. "Funny" does not mean "bad" (as in spoiled), or "different" (as in wild rabbit). Rotten meat gives off the sickly-sweet scent of bacteria, and the meat will look slimy and feel mushy. Like all small game, freshly-skinned wild rabbits smell like concentrated versions of the wild plants they've been munching such as milkweed and thistle, plants that humans can't digest directly, wherefore our noses react with suspicion to their odor. But the meat will be springy to the touch, look healthy, and taste good, and it won't smell "funny." It will just smell different.

When venison smells "funny," and that pronouncement is accompanied by a crinkled nose and a scrunched brow, it's often due to the addition of sex pheromones that bucks use to announce they're in the mood for love. If a chef experimentally adds a dash of Old Spice to the pork chops in order to achieve a certain je ne sais quoi, the results will be technically edible but not delicious. The same holds true of venison infused with eau de buck.

Solution: Make sure to keep hands and tools very clean while gutting and skinning a buck. It can be partly helped in cooking by the use of strong spices such as rosemary, garlic, or cumin.

It's just…off.

The mystery bad flavor in venison is usually the fat. In turn, the "bad" flavor of deer fat is a function of their diet.

If the deer are eating acorns, tannin builds up in their fat. Tannin is used to tan hides. It is highly acidic and poisonous to humans. Acorns are very nutritious, so the people of Appalachia, the *Foxfire* oral history project tells us, used to let their hogs run feral in the woods so they could root on the ground for them. Two weeks before slaughtering, the hogs would be rounded up and "finished" with a diet of corn, which is not only high in sugar but full of fat (wherefore corn oil). This diet purged their valuable fat of the sharp, bitter taste of the tannins found in acorns.

If your deer is an early fall country deer mostly eating farmed corn, its fat will taste fine. If your deer is a winter forest deer and mostly eating wild acorns, its fat will taste terrible. If you are unsure what your deer has been eating, slice off a piece of fat, toss it in a skillet, fry it up, and taste it.

Should you be so lucky to come across a plump doe that's been gorging on blueberries and feral apples for weeks and months, the hindquarters will be thickly padded with fat as thick as mutton, just like the *White House Cookbook* says. This fat will be fluffy, shiny fat that goes translucent when cooked, and best served warm so the fat stays loose. It is not to be confused with suet, a dry, crumbly fat that looks like dried spackling and sticks to everything. Though beef suet is essential to many British dessert recipes and makes an unbeatable piecrust, venison suet never tastes good to humans. Trim it and give it to the chickadees.

Whether suet or fluff, fat turns rancid with relative swiftness. This is one of the reasons why it's generally recommended to consume wild meat within three months of freezing. Because many subsistence hunters put venison in the freezer in order to live off it until the next hunting season rolls around, it's entirely possible that the fat will have turned rancid during that period of approximately eleven months. Most home butchering manuals thus recommend that every scrap of fat be trimmed off the venison before preserving, because it also tends to absorb bad flavors if it is left to hang while still in the hide.

Solution: If the fat is sweet, consume while fresh. But any venison intended for the freezer should be trimmed of all fat before going in.

It's tougher than shoe leather.
In addition to the problems of cold shortening, rigor mortis, and failure to hang for a sufficient length of time, roast-

ing will produce this result if tried on most cuts of venison unless it is heavily larded. Incomplete trimming will also produce this effect, as sautéed venison that has not been ruthlessly trimmed of its "silver skin" (a membranous sheath holding muscles together) will be chewy. Finally, overcooking will always produce a tough piece of venison.

Roasting: It doesn't matter if the roasting is done at home in an oven or spit-turned over a campfire. Roasting is dry heat that pulls moisture from the food cooking in the pan. "Moisture" specifically means water content. On the cellular level, water is a major component of all organic matter. When the cellular bonds begin to break from high heat, H_2O—water—gets released. Some of this forms steam. Some of this released moisture results in drippings, which is water freed from the cells combined with liquefied fat. Roasting, and especially roasting without a lid, means that all the moisture will dissipate through sustained heat, and leave behind a dry, tough piece of meat.

To discourage this outcome, factory-farmed birds and livestock are heavily watered to plump up the cells, even as they are fed soybeans and corn to fatten them by the most direct means possible: by feeding them fatty foods such as soybean and corn (soybeans make "vegetable oil," and corn makes "corn oil"). Before packaging, commercially produced poultry birds are routinely injected with "flavor," adding water, sugar (dextrose), and salt into the breasts to further ensure that conventional roasting will not dry out the white meat, which is the leanest part of the bird. By contrast, wild animals are neither regularly watered nor given feed, and their diet is typically wild fruits, berries, seeds, and green plants with almost no fats. Wild venison is thus always lower in moisture and leaner than farmed meat, including farmed venison. Despite the fact that a venison rump cut can look exactly like a beef rump roast, it will not cook up the same way, no matter how much you want to believe that this time it will be different. No, it won't.

Basting makes the cook feel useful but it does not magically reintroduce lost water back into the cells, and it doesn't do much except make the meat temporarily look shiny. The goal is to keep the juices—that is, the "moisture"—from exiting the meat in the first place. This is best accomplished by resisting the urge to roast it.

Sautéing refers to quick-cooking food using a small amount of oil in a very hot, flat pan. The word, sauté, means "jump": the point is to keep the food moving. This method of cooking ought to work on wild meat. Sometimes it does, but more often it ends up contracting fibers, producing toughness. This is because "very hot" means higher heats than many home cooks are comfortable using, out of reasonable fear of causing fires. This happens when the oil in the pan has a low flash point, but even oils that have a high flash point will smoke when approaching the "high" temperatures required. Meat cooks so rapidly using this method that overcooking is common.

Overcooking can result from several factors, including 1) too long in heat, 2) not enough fat and 3) not enough moisture. It also happens when the cook forgets to set the timer or forgets that meat continues to "cook" after being removed from heat.

Overcooking meat is a common problem, and it is generally motivated by a fear of pathogens. "Pathogens" sounds scary, but it's a catchall term for infectious agents, chiefly microorganisms such as bacteria and viruses, that cause diseases. From a food safety perspective, ground meats should be cooked thoroughly, meaning until there is no pink. However, quality cuts that have been correctly handled are not exposed to grinder blades or oxygen, and are thus less likely to spoil. Gain confidence by using a meat thermometer. Internal temperatures should reach 160°F.

Solution: Don't roast. Braise. If sautéing, work at high heats very quickly.

It tastes like bacon.
This is because the venison is draped in bacon.

The theory behind this practice is straightforward: because wild meat lacks the rind of fat and the marbling of beef, the cook cleverly replaces it with strips of fat that comes from a handy pig. As the venison roasts in the oven, the bacon fat will melt into the meat, keeping it moist and flavorful. It is a good theory, but doesn't work for those too nearsighted to thread a needle. For the "bacon" method to produce good results, the cook shoves little cubes of pure pork fat called "lardons" into tiny incisions made all around the surface, spacing them about one inch apart, and using a larding needle to draw the fat through. This method dates back to at least the 16th century. As advised by *A Proper newe Booke of Cokerye,* "Take nothynge but pepper and salte, but lette it haue ynoughe, and yf the Veneson be leane, larde it throughe wyth bacon." Alternately, one can "bard" the roast, which requires an ingredient that is more or less impossible to get in the United States: this is caul, a lacy web of fat removed from the pig's intestines and wrapped around the roast.

Five centuries ago, in other words, cooks were wrestling with the problem of what to do with chewy venison. They fixed it by adding lots of pure pig fat (which is not bacon) and tying it to the roast. The poor man's version of larding and barding, which is now pretty much everybody's version, involves wrapping the venison in strips of bacon to fashion a second skin that is either tied or sewn in place before roasting. Both methods are a lot of work and, frankly, I find it weird to sew bacon to raw meat. Also, every recipe I have ever read for this approach fails to mention that the roast has to be covered for the entire period except the final ten minutes, or else the bacon will be burned long before your venison is cooked. Even if the roast does come out tender and juicy, your venison will taste like bacon, and your bacon will be too rubbery to enjoy. If you want bacon, fry up some bacon. Leave the venison out of it.

Solution: Don't use bacon. Or, if the urge cannot be resisted, use high quality, nitrate-free, uncured bacon, which will prevent that salty taste from infusing the meat.

It's mushy and *tough.*

If the carcass froze before cooling, a mushy texture results. Or, it was left too long in a marinade, and then overcooked.

The theory on marinades is that they tenderize tough meat. They do, but only to a very limited point. Marinades that have acidic ingredients such as tomato, vinegar, wine, soy sauce, or Worcestershire sauce, tenderize meat by breaking protein bonds while attracting water molecules, facilitating the intra-cellular retention of moisture. The effect of this, eating-wise, is the perception of tenderness. But if left too long in a marinade, the newly formed water bonds break and the fibers bind up again, creating toughness. Other marinades that feature pineapple and yogurt utilize enzymes to break down the meat in much the same way as its own natural process, but the same limitations apply, and mushiness can result. Traditional recipes that call for a very long marinade time, up to three days, usually precede stewing, meaning that they expect the meat to collapse and dissolve into a liquid.

It is also the case that a marinade can only penetrate red meat a few millimeters, so this step will do little to tenderize a round cut or a thick steak. Thus, marinades are best understood as a vehicle to add flavor to the venison. A marinade consisting of oils or fats helps seasonings penetrate the muscle fibers, and ultimately can greatly enhance the dish.

Solution: Limit the time the meat rests in the marinade, and consider it a way to add flavor, not to make it tender. For flank steaks, steaks, and thinly sliced rounds, pound to tenderize by using a meat mallet.

CHAPTER FIVE
Recipes

In his 2013 book, *The Devouring Dragon,* reporter Craig Simon describes his culinary adventures in China, including his reaction to venison from a wildlife sanctuary in Sichuan province.

> An official happy to be hosting an American guest presented me with a plate of what he said was a wild local deer. He told me it had been killed in the park and was healthier than farm-raised animals. To maintain our friendship, I took a few bites of the tough, gamey meat.

Politely, he pushed the rest aside. Scenarios like this are common, leading to venison's reputation as gasoline-flavored shoe leather. Choking down venison out of a sense of obligation, whether to the host or to the animal, is a dismal outcome that leaves a bad taste behind. How to avoid this tragedy in the kitchen?

The answer lies in cooking methods that enhance the qualities of the meat rather than hiding the taste. Smothering a quality piece of meat in cream of mushroom soup or barbecue sauce should be reserved for the unavoidable disasters. Because there will be unavoidable disasters. It's not always the case that an ideal buck gets served for supper.

Some people don't enjoy venison. The most perfect preparation can't alter the basic dynamics of personal chemistry. It's not a question of whether or not a particular food tastes good. It's a question of whether the food tastes good *to you*. A palate that finds farm-raised lamb too strongly flavored will react similarly to venison. Indeed, because of its richer concentration of tastes, lamb is often described as being "gamy."

Alternative wild options with different flavor profiles are turkey, grouse, and small game in general. Game birds don't have pheromones, so "gamy" flavors are less likely to be a problem. Because they start out so much smaller than deer, they are also simpler to dress, and easier to physically handle in the kitchen. However, small game presents special culinary challenges because their sex and age impacts their cooking. With turkeys, it's not so hard to determine if it's a gobbler or a hen but … doe rabbits versus buck rabbits? It's not exactly obvious. The cook must become a zoologist with a basic grasp of natural history, for a young female rabbit and an old male rabbit are, from the cook's perspective, different animals.

× WHAT'S THE STORY?

Every hunt is a story. Sometimes, it's a story of venison. With industrial meat, the story is always the same, a tragic tale of predestination where everybody dies young. With wild game, by contrast, the story is always different, ranging from high adventure to farce, and good fun even when it's not. In London, a restaurant called The Story specializes in wild game, connecting the conversation that comes out of the mouth to

Stag with lowered head is meeting the charge of a mounted knight; illustration of a fable by Aesop. Credit: Wellcome Institute.

the venison that goes in. The venison's goodness is directly linked to the story of the hunt, because the details of how the hunt unfurled directly impact its preparation. If the venison had to be rescued, this is best known before, rather than after, guests sit down at the table.

Even if you were the one doing the hunting, there's usually more than one point of view to consider, including the deer's, which ought to be acknowledged since it's getting eaten. The truer the account, the better the venison. Too often, instead of addressing the slog and the frustration, popular narratives like to celebrate chest-beating fantasies of inner cavemen, even as the imagination turns thoughts of hale camaraderie combined with a sense of lost nobility. Which is fine to indulge, until it ends up ruining supper.

The most stubborn myth of all is the haunch of venison spit roasted over a roaring fire, as King Arthur's knights clank their goblets and tear manfully into their quarry. Today's knights wear UnderArmor™ thermal underwear and ride ATVs instead of Arabian stallions, but they still insist on roasting the venison the "real" way by shoving it into a fire or over a bed of hot coals. Unfortunately, actual knights didn't cook their venison that way, because they had vassals, squires, and cooks to prepare it for them.

Dated around 1375, a famous collection of recipes by a French cook named Taillevent provides a set of directions for preparing "fresh" stag (male red deer) and wild boar. As with all recipes from this period, these directions are somewhat cryptic, but they basically recommended that the entire creature be parboiled very quickly (dipped in boiling hot water for one or two minutes, a step that would have killed surface pathogens), then coated thickly with lard and boiled in wine. Alternately, it could be parboiled, covered in lard, set in a pasty, spiced, and then roasted. Both versions were served with "Cameline" sauce, which consisted of ginger, cassia [close to cinnamon], cloves, grains of paradise [paprika, cardamom, and black pepper], mastic thyme [(*Thymus mastichina*), Spanish wood marjoram], and black pepper, to which was added grilled bread soaked in wine and vinegar. This mixture was then placed in a cheesecloth, strained, and salted to taste.

Over the centuries, French and English cooks continued to prepare venison in a similar fashion, helping us fill in the steps that Taillevent didn't record. In John Murrell's *New booke of Cookerie; London Cookerie*, 1615, the "redde Deere," or stag, was prepared thus:

> Parboyle it, and presse it, and let it lye all night in redde Wine, and vinegar: then Lard it thicke, and season it with Pepper, Salt, Cloves, Mace, Nutmeg, and Ginger. Bake it in a deepe Coffin of Rye-paste, with store of Butter: let it soake well. Leave a vent-hole in your Pye, and when you draw it out of the Oven, put in melted Butter, Vinegar, Nutmeg, Ginger, and a little Sugar: shake it very well together, and put it into the Oven againe, and let it stand three or foure houres at the least, to soake throughly, when your Oven is colde take it out, and stop the hole with Butter.

It retained the 14th-century convention of parboiling but added the step of "pressing," which is a method still used with curing hams in order to get all the blood out of it. The venison was marinated overnight at room temperature in red wine and vinegar, then coated all over in lard, seasoned with salt, pepper, cloves, mace, nutmeg, and ginger, then wrapped up in a thick paste made of rye flour and lots of butter, making sure to leave a little hole to serve as a vent. It was baked until the crust became hard, then the cook poured melted butter, vinegar, nutmeg, ginger, and sugar into the vent, shook the whole thing to make sure these ingredients covered the venison, and then baked it again for another three or four hours at low heat as the woodstove burned down.

When haunches were roasted, in other words, they were protected by a heavy layer of lard and a flour paste "coffin" that hardened as it baked for three to four hours. Two centuries later, the *White House Cookbook* offered a buttered variation of Murrell's "coffin" method, which is a lot of effort but has certain advantages if using a woodstove, which would have been the case for chefs of all levels until the mid-20th century. For cooks using a modern electric or gas stove, braising is a much simpler way to achieve comparable results with a large roast or haunch of venison. Bluntly, the *White House Cookbook* stated: "Venison should never be roasted unless very fat." And it *would* have been very fat if it was an autumn doe that had been gorging itself all summer without fear of predators. But it still didn't recommend that the fattest of haunches be roasted. The only cut that might be treated this way was the now-defunct saddle, and only then by first covering it entirely with thick strips of salt pork to "lard" it.

The story of venison is thus also a story of pigs, the source of much of the fat used to make the venison juicy. For survival and for pleasure, the need for fat is a constant theme that embeds venison inside a domestic system of livestock, cooks, and diners, where the wild animal is a surprise guest of honor supported by local, small-scale agriculture. By the time the deer gets butchered into cuts, wrapped in paper, and labeled for the freezer, it's easy to forget that these small packages used to be a wild animal. But as long as there are conversations around the dinner table, its story will not be forgotten. What follows here is a discussion of the best cooking methods for the particular cut, with the goal of ensuring tender and tasty results.

× RECIPES

The simplest recipes are the best. When the venison is sweet and tender, it only needs the correct cooking method for the cut, clarified butter, sea salt and good black pepper, and a bit of currant jelly sauce to accompany it.

Sauces, gravies, and jellies made of ingredients that are part of the deer's natural diet tend to partner well with venison.

These include currants, blueberries, blackberries, and red berries (raspberry, cranberry, elderberry) and the classic pairing, currants. Mushroom sauces are also good, and many cooks favor marinades using red wine and dry rubs with cocoa, black pepper, and hot red peppers such as chili.

Backstraps and Tenderloins. Pan Sear or Grill.
Haunch with bone in. Braise.
Haunch, deboned, cut into rounds, steaks, kebabs or strips. Marinate, sear over high heat, and sauté or grill very quickly.
Neck: Pot roast or Stew.
Shoulder: Braise or Long Marinade.
Shanks: Crockpot or Slow Stew.
Scraps: Mincemeat or Grind.

Use a quality skillet. A well-seasoned, 16" cast iron skillet or stainless steel skillet will adapt to any number of jobs. Never use nonstick. A thin, cheap frying pan will burn your venison. Electric frying pans will do in a pinch but the results will not be as good.

Invest in a large roasting pan with a lid. Braising haunches and shoulders is the most reliable method of cooking tender venison. A large roaster will make the job easier.

Always rinse and dry the venison for 2-4 hours before cooking, and if possible, let it air dry overnight in the refrigerator. Dry meat will respond better to a marinade and will also caramelize nicely.

If browning or sautéing, make sure the pan is very hot. Conventional wisdom says that "hot enough" is when you fling a drop of water at the pan and it immediately evaporates.

Use clarified butter (ghee) or an oil that can withstand high temperatures. These include good quality canola and grapeseed oil.

But ghee is preferred, as butter and red meat is an unbeatable combination.

Let it rest. Braised and pan-seared venison should be removed from heat and allowed to sit quietly for about ten minutes before serving.

× THE ONE RECIPE THAT WORKS FOR EVERYTHING: BRAISED HAUNCH OF VENISON

This recipe will work on all cuts of venison, and should be used when the cook doesn't have any information on the animal. The water at the bottom of the pan is meant to steam, not boil the meat. Don't immerse the cut, and don't check it too often. Be careful when you lift the lid, as steam will rush out and can swiftly burn.

Trim all suet from the haunch. Rinse in warm water, or wipe with a clean moist cloth. Pat dry, and, if possible, leave uncovered to air dry in the refrigerator overnight. Massage the haunch with extra virgin olive oil and chopped garlic. Place in roaster, add as much hot water as required to create a shallow depth of ½ inch, and cover with a tight lid. (If you don't have a lid, cover the top with a sheet of heavy duty tin foil and seal tightly.) Cook at 300°F for 3-4 hours until the meat is tender, checking hourly, adding fresh boiling water as it reduces. When meat is done, it will pull away from the bone. Finish by removing the cover and letting the top brown for 10 minutes. Remove from heat and let rest for 15 minutes. Carve and serve with currant jelly or cranberry sauce.

× RECIPES FOR TOUGH VENISON

When the animal is old, it's practical to just skip the guesswork and go straight for the grinder. Mixed with beef and pork, tough venison makes acceptable hamburgers and sausages. But many traditional recipes also do the trick, because farmers couldn't afford to waste a single scrap. These traditional recipes call for an old, tough animal; if you try it on a young one, you'll end up with marinade soup.

× **VENISON POT ROAST**

Ingredients
> 5-6 pounds venison (rump roast from large buck)
> 1 sweet onion, chopped
> 1 t salt
> 1 t black pepper
> 4 T butter
> 1 T cornstarch

Wash venison and set inside a Dutch oven. Add cold water until barely covered. Bring to a boil, reduce quickly, and let simmer for an hour. Add chopped onions, salt, and pepper, and resume simmering until tender (about three hours). Let the liquids reduce but do not let it boil down. Remove meat and set aside. Pour out the liquids and set aside. Add butter, bring the heat up to medium high, and when the butter begins to brown, return meat to pot and brown it on all sides, turning frequently. Take ¼ cup of the liquid and sprinkle it with the cornstarch, whisking it until there are no lumps and the consistency is even. Add this mixture to the remaining liquid and whisk until it's smooth. Remove the meat and plate it. Pour the cornstarch and liquid back into the Dutch oven, and warm on low heat until it thickens into a gravy. Remove from heat and pour into a gravy dish. Serve both hot, the meat on a platter.

× **BREADED VENISON STEAKS**

Ingredients
> 4 venison steaks
> Salt and pepper
> 1 egg, well beaten
> 1 C panko crumbs

¼ C clarified butter
1 t flour
¼ C hot water
1 t currant jelly

Put clarified butter in skillet on high heat. Pound venison steaks with a meat mallet until thin. Rub both sides with salt and pepper. Dip in beaten egg and place immediately in bread crumbs, pressing down to make sure both sides are well covered, then lay on hot skillet. Brown both sides quickly (about 3 minutes per side), then cover and keep on low for 20 minutes. Remove steaks from the pan, toss the flour into the remaining butter to make a roux, then add hot water and currant jelly to make a sauce.

× **POT AU FEU**

This is a recipe for cooking meat "bad in quality" that the hunter has "gotten" in the field, from Peter Hawker, *Instructions to Young Sportsmen*, 1830. Though Hawker doesn't give his dish a name, it's a recipe for the classic French dish *Pot au feu*. Translated literally, it means "pot on the fire," and came into being around 1660 as a peasant dish fit for a king. The key ingredient is a large piece of red meat that requires long, slow cooking.

There is but one good and easy way of dressing. This I shall now translate from my French recipe: viz. Let your servant take Three pounds of meat, a large carrot, two onions, and two turnips. (The Frenchman adds also a cabbage: here John Bull [i.e., English version of "John Doe," a generic man of his country] may please himself.) Put them into two quarts of water, to simmer away till reduced to three pints. Let him season the soup to the taste, with pepper, salt, herbs, &c. &c. He must then cut off square about a pound of the fattest part of the meat, and put it aside, letting the rest boil completely to pieces. After he has well skimmed off the fat, and strained the soup, let him put

it by till wanted. On your return, while seeing your
dogs fed, which every sportsman ought to do, Let you
like to have them, and, for the last ten minutes, boil
again the square piece of meat which was reserved.
Another necessary part of the recipe also should be
prescribed, lest the dish should fall into disrepute. To
prevent the deputy cook from helping himself, and
filling it up with water, let him have a partnership
in the concern; and when he has occasion to quit the
room, he should either lock the door, or leave one of
your relay dogs for a sentry. You will then have a good
wholesome gravy soup to begin with; and, afterwards,
some tender meat, which if [you] Eat with mustard,
a little raw parsley chopped fine, and a few anchovies,
you will, it is presumed, find an excellent dish.

Should you not have servants to do your cooking in the field,
here is a classic recipe for Pot au Feu, modified for venison.

Ingredients
3–4 pounds of venison (round or shoulder, trimmed)
1 carrot
2 onions
2 white turnips
4 leeks or a head of cabbage
2 t sea salt
1 t black pepper
Fresh flat or curly parsley, chopped

Place venison in a large pot, add enough water to cover, bring to
a boil. Skim off any scum that rises to the surface. Continue to
boil until no more scum forms. Add salt, pepper, and the peeled
carrots and turnips, cut into 1 inch cubes. Peel and trim leeks.
Bundle together and place in liquid. Add chopped fresh parsley,
reduce heat and simmer for two hours. Remove meat and serve
hot or cold, with hot leeks and root vegetables on the side.

× **SAUERBRATEN**

In German, "sauerbraten" means sour roast meat. It is one of the national dishes of Germany and is an excellent way to prepare tough venison, including venison that is gamy. The long marinating time helps the strong marinade penetrate the venison, masking the taste and odors associated with gaminess, and the slow cooking method produces tender meat. Sauerbraten is identical to hasenpfeffer except that instead of a tough, old, wild rabbit, it features a tough chunk of red meat.

Ingredients
- 3-4 pounds of venison (whole rump or whole neck roast from a large buck)
- 1 C dry red wine
- 1 C apple cider vinegar
- 1 C water
- 1 T sea salt
- 2 T ground cloves
- 1 T crushed juniper berries
- 6 bay leaves
- 2 yellow onions, sliced

Step One: Marinating. Time: 2-3 days.
Put red wine, vinegar, water, salt, cloves, juniper berries, bay leaves, and onions in a saucepan, bring to a boil, and let cool to room temperature. Place venison in a nonreactive bowl with a lid, pour cooled mixture over the meat, and let marinate in the refrigerator for three days, turning occasionally.

Step Two: Cooking

Ingredients
- 3-6 T butter
- ¼ C white sugar
- 1 T ground ginger

Remove venison from marinade. Strain marinade through a sieve, discarding onions and spices, add ¼ cup of sugar to the liquid, and set aside. Place meat in colander over sink, let drain, and pat dry.

Place the Dutch oven on the stove, set to medium high, let it get hot, then toss in three to five tablespoons of butter. When butter bubbles and just starts to brown, place the dry meat in the butter and brown on all sides. Once meat is browned and caramelized, slowly add all the reserved marinade. Add a tablespoon of ground ginger. Bring to a low boil, reduce heat, then cover the Dutch oven with a tight lid. Let it simmer for 2-3 hours, stirring occasionally, until the meat is tender enough to cut with a fork. Remove and serve with the liquid sauce. Sauerbraten is traditionally served with a side of red cabbage.

× **SPICY VENISON STEW**

This method is ideal for preparing the shoulders and front shanks of smaller deer (under 125 pounds), which are difficult to debone without sacrificing a lot of good meat. It also works well with neck meat or any tough buck. Though this recipe is long, it's not as complicated as it seems. The caramelized onions can be prepared ahead. The braising can also be done ahead and the pulled meat refrigerated until needed. The flavors are complex and surprisingly sophisticated. This makes a meal fit for company.

Ingredients
  1 venison shoulder (bone-in)
  Dry rub (1 T garlic salt, 1 t chili powder, and ½ t black pepper)
  2 cups hot water, plus more as needed
  2 T extra virgin olive oil or good butter, plus more as needed
  5 large sweet white onions, sliced thinly

Pinch of salt and pepper
3 T extra virgin olive oil or good butter
3 T dark brown sugar
5 t chopped garlic or 1 head of garlic, smashed and chopped
1 t sea salt
3 T Moroccan Seasoning (Ras El Hanout)
1 T chili powder (optional)

Set oven to 300°F. Take one whole venison shoulder with shank, bone in. Rinse, being sure to remove all stray hairs and bone chips. Pat dry with paper towels. Massage with a few drops of olive oil, then add a dry rub of garlic salt, chili powder, and black pepper. Place in large roasting pan or rimmed cookie tray, add hot water to a ½ inch depth, cover tightly with lid or baking foil, and place carefully in oven. Set timer for 1 hour.

In a large sauté pan, place 2 T of butter or olive oil and heat on medium, add the onions, bring the heat down to low, and stir. The slices will become translucent after about 15-20 minutes. Turn the heat up slightly and keep stirring, adding more butter or oil as necessary to keep them moving. After an additional 20 minutes, the slices will be mushy and golden brown. Bring heat back to low and keep stirring. In another 20 minutes, the onions will be the consistency of applesauce. Add a pinch of sea salt and black pepper, stir in, remove from pan, and set aside. Caramelizing the onions can be done a day ahead.

It is now 1 hour later. Check the shoulder, making sure that there is still water on bottom of the roasting pan (Be careful: lifting the lid will release steam. Wear oven mitts and don't put your face near the roasting pan.) If it is low, add more hot water. Then cover, return to oven, and set timer for 1 hour.

Place 2-3 T of butter or olive oil into a large heavy skillet, medium heat, until the butter is melted or oil is loose. Add brown sugar and stir briskly to make a smooth, heavy paste. Add the caramelized sweet onions, salt, garlic, and Moroccan seasonings, plus 1/2 cup hot water or until the mixture is the consistency of loose gravy. Turn up heat and stir briskly until the mixture is just starting to boil. Reduce heat to lowest possible setting and let simmer, stirring occasionally. As it thickens, add more water to loosen the liquid again. Do not let the sauce boil down.

It is now 1 hour later. Check roast for doneness. If it is sufficiently cooked, the meat will be pulling away from the bone. (If not, place back in oven for an additional hour.) Remove from oven, place on large chopping board, and let rest until it is cool enough to handle. The meat should pull cleanly off the bones and be very tender. Chop into regular-sized pieces and place them in the sauce. Add more water, stir, cover pan, and let simmer for another half hour until the sauce has thickened. For those who prefer more spice, add chili powder at this time. Remove from heat and serve over basmati rice. Serves six.

× SPICY VENISON STEW, VERSION 2

A faster version of the same recipe works for 3-4 pounds of venison, cubed (especially good for neck meat). When cubing: Cut the venison into 1-2 inch cubes; the idea is to have the pieces be as close in size as possible. Wash, rinse, pat dry, and set aside.

Ingredients
    3-4 pounds of venison, cubed (neck meat and flank)
    Pinch of salt and pepper, to taste
    5 t chopped garlic or 1 head of garlic, smashed and chopped, adding more to taste
    2 T extra virgin olive oil or good butter, plus more as needed
    Pinch of salt and pepper, to taste
    5 large sweet white onions, sliced thinly
    3 T extra virgin olive oil or good butter
    3 T dark brown sugar
    1 t sea salt
    3 T Moroccan Seasoning (Ras El Hanout)
    1 T chili powder (optional)

Place the cubed venison in a stainless steel bowl with garlic, salt, and pepper, stirring to make sure that all sides are coated, and marinate in the refrigerator for 2 hours.

Caramelize the onions as above: In a large sauté pan, place 2 T of olive oil or butter and heat on medium, add the onions, bring the heat down to low, and stir. The slices will become translucent after about 15-20 minutes. Turn the heat up slightly and keep stirring, adding more oil or butter as necessary to keep them moving. After an additional 20 minutes, the slices will be mushy and golden brown. Bring heat back to low and keep stirring. In another 20 minutes, the onions will be the consistency of applesauce. Add a pinch of sea salt and black pepper, stir in, remove from pan, and set aside.

Place 2-3 T of butter or olive oil into a large heavy skillet, medium heat, until the butter is melted or oil is loose. Add brown sugar and stir briskly so the sugar and butter make a smooth, heavy paste. Add the caramelized sweet onions and all the seasonings, plus ½ cup hot water. Bring to just boiling, stirring briskly until the mixture is the consistency of a loose gravy. Stir in the cubed meat, making sure that that there is at least ½ inch of sauce in the pan. If not, add more water and bring back to just boiling. Set on low, cover skillet, and simmer for forty minutes to an hour, stirring occasionally. The sauce should be the consistency of a rich gravy and the meat should be fork-tender. Remove from heat and serve over basmati rice. Serves six.

× MOROCCAN SEASONING (RAS EL HANOUT)

This seasoning is a mixture of cumin, cardamom, mace, ginger, turmeric, coriander, paprika, cinnamon, black pepper, white pepper, and other spices. Premixed versions are available in larger chain grocery stores. If not, just make your own. It is an excellent dry rub for venison as well.

Ingredients
>   2 t ground ginger
>   2 t ground cardamom
>   2 t ground mace
>   1 t sugar
>   1 t cinnamon
>   1 t ground allspice
>   1 t ground coriander seeds
>   1 t ground nutmeg
>   1 t turmeric
>   ½ t ground black pepper
>   ½ t ground white pepper
>   ½ t ground cayenne pepper
>   ½ t ground anise seeds
>   ¼ t ground cloves

Mix together well. Store in airtight container.

× **VENISON SHANKS WITH LENTILS**

Considered a "cheap" cut, the shank isn't given much respect. Rock-hard before cooking, venison shanks are often ground up immediately for sausages and burgers. When braised or boiled, however, shanks become flavorful and tender, full of collagen that contributes to an almost creamy texture.

Ingredients
>   4 venison shanks
>   3 T flour (for gluten-free variation, omit the flour)
>   1 t cinnamon
>   1 t allspice
>   1/4 t salt
>   2 t curry powder
>   4 T oil
>   12 ounces of dried green lentils (preferably Lentilles du Puy*)

2 carrots, chopped
1 onion, chopped
1 T minced garlic
1 t dried thyme
2 bay leaves
1 bottle dry red wine

Wash shanks and pat dry. Mix together dry ingredients (flour, cinnamon, salt, allspice, and curry) and coat shanks. In a large oven-suitable skillet or Dutch oven, put in 4 T of oil and bring to high heat. As soon as the pan is hot, carefully put in shanks and brown on all sides. Turn off heat, cover, and let stand on burner for ten minutes. Remove shanks and set aside. Preheat oven to 400°F.

On stovetop, bring burner heat back up to high. Using same skillet or Dutch oven, place carrots, onions, and garlic in the drippings and the hot fat, adding more if necessary. Sauté for 5 minutes, until the garlic is fragrant and the onions are just becoming translucent. Add lentils, thyme, bay leaves, and wine. Stir to combine. Bring to boil on top of stove, place shanks among this mixture, cover the pan with lid or heavy foil, and place in oven. Lower the heat to 350° and cook for 1 hour.

Uncover, stir, sprinkle with salt and pepper, recover and cook for another hour until the shanks are tender and begins to pull away from the bone. Check periodically to make sure the mixture isn't drying out. If necessary, add water. When venison is tender, uncover, turn off the oven and broil at at 400° until the top is browned, about ten minutes. Serve with roasted red potatoes.

*Sometimes called "peasant's caviar," Lentilles du Puy are a French green lentil, smaller and darker than conventional green lentils. They are uniquely flavored and will hold their shape after long periods of cooking. Because they are so desirable, copycats will be labeled "French Lentils," or something similar, but authentic Lentilles du Puy will be marked "AOC" on the packaging. They are expensive, but truly worth it.

× <u>**VENISON IN THAI GREEN CURRY**</u>

Ingredients
>4 venison shanks
>Salt and pepper
>3 T butter
>2 T Thai green curry paste
>1 can coconut milk
>1 C chicken stock, plus more as needed
>2 T brown sugar
>1 cup frozen corn
>1 package flat rice sticks, medium thickness ("pad thai noodle." A standard package is about 16 oz.)

Clean shanks and place them in a medium pot. Cover with water, bring to a boil, reduce heat and simmer until tender, approximately 2 hours. Remove from heat, pull off meat and mince. Place in bowl, toss with salt and pepper, and set aside.

Using a pot large enough to hold eight-ten cups of water, bring to a boil, remove from heat, and soak noodles for six minutes. When ready, noodles will be soft but chewy. (Do not let them sit for longer than eight minutes, or they will become mushy.) Meanwhile, in a large sauté pan, warm up butter on medium heat, add curry sauce and brown sugar, and stir until mixed. Add chicken stock and stir until mixed, then add coconut milk. Stir together and bring to a boil. Reduce heat immediately to low. The sauce should be creamy but not as thick as gravy. Taste. Those who like more heat should add more green curry at this time. Add frozen corn, and stir for five minutes at low heat. Add venison, stir to coat, then add noodles to the pan, and toss thoroughly. Remove and serve warm.

× **VENISON IN THAI GREEN CURRY, VERSION 2**

Ingredients
  2-3 pounds venison flank or shoulder
  Marinade (1 t Thai green curry paste, 1 t corn oil, 2 T
  lemon juice, 1 t brown sugar)
  2-3 T butter
  1 T Thai green curry paste
  2 T brown sugar
  1 C chicken stock, plus more as needed
  1 red pepper, sliced
  1 can baby corn
  1 can bamboo shoots

Start by slicing or shaving meat across the grain. Stretching
the meat makes it easy to see which way the grain runs. Then
cut across the grain, in the manner of slicing up a tree trunk.
If you cut with the grain, in the manner of splitting wood,
long stringy pieces will result. Marinate the slices in 1 t Thai
green curry paste mixed with 1 t oil, 2 T lemon juice, and 1 t
brown sugar. Place in refrigerator for 2 hours.

In a large sauté pan, add butter and heat until bubbling.
Add sliced red pepper and stir, keeping the pepper moving,
taking care that it doesn't burn. When it has begun to soften (about five minutes), add drained baby corn and bamboo
shoots, and keep stirring another five minutes. Remove vegetables from pan, set aside. Add venison to hot pan and sear
quickly. Remove meat from the pan.

Using a pot large enough to hold eight-ten cups of water, bring to a boil, remove from heat, and soak noodles for
eight minutes (if the water isn't enough to cover, add more
hot water until submerged). Meanwhile, in the sauté pan, add
1 T curry paste and brown sugar, and stir until mixed. Add
chicken stock and stir until mixed, then add coconut milk.
Stir together and bring to a boil. Reduce heat immediately to

low. The sauce should be creamy but not as thick as gravy. Taste. Add venison, stir to coat, then add noodles to the pan, toss thoroughly. Add vegetables, and toss. Remove and serve warm. Serves four.

× **VENISON BULGOGI**

Bulgogi is one of the most famous traditional dishes of Korea. It is a marinade preparation usually made with beef and cooked over a special small grill. Kimchi is now widely available in most grocery stores; it is usually found in the refrigerated produce section. This preparation freezes well in marinade, which slowly tenderizes the thinly sliced meat.

Ingredients
> 2 pounds venison flank steak or similar cut (ribeye, steak)
> 1 T vegetable oil
> ⅓ C soy sauce
> 3 T white sugar
> 2 T sesame oil
> 2 cloves of garlic, minced
> 1 yellow onion, sliced very thin
> 2 green onions, finely chopped
> 1 T toasted sesame seeds
> 1 t red pepper flakes
> Pinch of black pepper
> 1 t ginger, finely minced

Dipping sauce
> ½ C soy sauce
> 2 T sesame oil
> 1 t minced green onion tops
> 1 t minced garlic
> 1 pinch black pepper

Start by thinly shaving the meat. If you don't have a shaver, slice the meat as thinly as possible, cutting across the grain, then spread it out on a cutting board, cover with a layer of plastic wrap, and pound with a meat mallet to break down the fibers. (If you don't cover it, little bits of meat will go flying around the room.) Pound energetically; it's okay if there are holes in the meat. Place in a nonreactive bowl, add oil, and toss to coat.

In a large nonreactive mixing bowl, combine all ingredients except the venison and onions. When most of the sugar has dissolved, add venison and onion slices to the bowl and mix well. Cover and refrigerate overnight.

Heat up a large sauté pan using high heat cooking oil. As soon as pan is very hot, place a few slices on the pan, laying them as flatly as possible. Using tongs or cooking chopsticks, turn when edges get crispy (it cooks almost instantly). Repeat until all the venison is cooked.

In a small mixing bowl, add all ingredients for sauce: soy sauce, sesame oil, green onions, garlic, and black pepper. Serve venison with white rice and kimchi, dipping sauce on the side. Serves four.

× VENISON IN SOUTH INDIAN SAUCES

These next two recipes for Venison Vindaloo and Venison Korma come from Tom Whyte, an anthropologist who specializes in the prehistory of the Appalachians and Zooarcheology. He lives and hunts in South Carolina. The spicy sauces are not only delicious, they help mask gamy flavors. Small chunks are pan fried and then braised in the oven.

× VENISON VINDALOO

Ingredients
  2 pounds bite-sized venison
  1 large onion
  4 oz. clarified butter or vegetable oil
  2 green chilis
  2 red chilis

4 garlic cloves
2 T ground coriander
2 t black pepper
1 t ground cumin
1 t ground turmeric
2 bay leaves
5 cloves
5 cardamoms
2 T vinegar
1 lemon
¾ pint boiling water
2-inch fresh ginger
2 t salt
1 T garam masala

Heat the oil and gently fry meat until sealed on both sides. Remove with slotted spoon and set aside.

To make the vindaloo paste, roast the bay leaves and cloves on a baking tray in a preheated oven at 400°F for 15 minutes. Meanwhile, chop the chili peppers and garlic, then grind these together with the coriander, cumin, turmeric, and black pepper. Remove the seeds from the cardamom and grind together with the roasted cloves and bay leaves. Mix them into the garlic and spice paste and add the vinegar. Squeeze in the juice from the lemon. Mix this paste in with the meat.

Reheat the remaining oil in a heavy saucepan. Peel and slice the onion and fry until just softening. Peel and slice thinly the ginger, add, and fry for another 2 minutes. Now add the meat with the paste and fry for a further 5 minutes. Pour in the boiling water and simmer for 40 minutes with pan tightly covered. Add garam masala and salt. Stir in well and simmer for 10-15 minutes until the meat is tender. Serve over basmati rice.

(If you use ground cloves and cardamom, use ¼ t cloves and ½ t cardamom. Chilis may be substituted with two or three seeded and ribbed jalapenos)

× VENISON KORMA

Ingredients
        2 pounds bite-sized venison
        1 medium onion chopped
        1 medium onion sliced
        4 oz. clarified butter or vegetable oil
        2 t fresh ginger grated
        2 red chilis
        3 garlic cloves roughly chopped
        1 T coriander seed
        2 t ground cumin
        1 t ground cardamom
        ½ t salt
        1 t chili flakes
        2 T ghee or clarified butter
        2 T tomato paste
        ½ C plain yogurt

Put chopped onion, ginger, garlic, coriander seeds, cumin, cardamom, salt, and chili flakes into a food processor and process
until a smooth paste forms. Add the spice mix to the venison
and stir well to coat. Set aside for one hour. Heat ghee in a large
heavy pan. Add the sliced onion and cook, stirring over moder-
ate heat until the onions soften. Add venison and cook for 8-10
minutes, stirring constantly, until browned all over. Add the
tomato paste and two teaspoons of the yogurt and stir until
combined. Simmer uncovered until the liquid is absorbed. Add
remaining yogurt, 2 tablespoons at a time, stirring between
each addition until the liquid is absorbed. Cover the pan and
simmer over low heat for 30 minutes, stirring occasionally.
Serve over basmati rice.

× WHAT TO DO WITH THE SCRAPS
With home butchering, there are always scraps. Some of the
scraps are ideal for grinding. Other scraps are terrific for

stews. Here are two options for cooking up the scraps that don't involve hamburger or meatballs.

× TAGLIATELLE WITH RICH THREE-MEAT SAUCE

This recipe has been shared by Rick and Jen, who run the popular website *Food for Hunters*. They live in the Midwest and their deer are generally corn-fed. For those looking for something new to try with ground venison, this is an excellent option.

Ingredients
- 4 T olive oil, extra for drizzling
- 3 oz. of pancetta (or lean bacon), diced
- 1 onion, chopped
- 1 garlic clove, minced
- 1 carrot, chopped
- 1 celery stalk, chopped
- ½ lb. ground venison
- ¼ C chicken liver, chopped
- 1 C of crushed tomatoes
- ½ C dry white wine, like Pinot Grigio or Chardonnay
- 1 C beef stock
- ½ t dried oregano
- 1 bay leaf
- 1 pound dried tagliatelle (pasta)
- Salt and pepper, to taste
- Grated Parmesan cheese, for serving

Over medium heat, heat 4 T of olive oil in a large heavy-bottom saucepan. Add chopped pancetta and cook for 3-5 minutes, or until just turning brown. Stir occasionally. Next, add chopped onion, carrot, celery and minced garlic. Cook for another 5 minutes, stirring occasionally. Then turn the heat up to high. Add ground venison and cook for 5 minutes, or until browned. Break up meat with a wooden spoon. After venison is browned, stir in chopped chicken liver. Cook for 2-3 minutes, stirring occasionally. Then, pour in 1 cup of beef stock and ½ cup of dry white wine. Add 1 cup of pureed tomatoes, oregano, and 1 bay leaf. Add salt and pepper, to taste. Bring to a boil, then reduce to a simmer. Cover and simmer for 30-45 minutes, or until sauce reaches desired thickness.

Meanwhile, bring a pot of lightly salted water to a boil. Add the tagliatelle pasta. Bring back to a boil. Cook according to package directions until tender but firm, al dente. Drain cooked pasta and transfer to a warm serving bowl. Drizzle with olive oil and toss well. Ladle sauce over pasta, toss again. Serve immediately with grated Parmesan.

× RUTH'S VENISON MINCEMEAT

Mincemeat is a very old dish that dates back to at least the 13th century. Formerly, it always included meat, and that meat was often venison. Specifically, it was red deer. Over the centuries, the meat disappeared, to be replaced with an all-fruit version, becoming a dessert instead of a meal. This old Maine recipe is a variation of a 19th-century British recipe. It seems fitting that a recipe that traveled from England to New England is now returned to its original form using venison. When baked into a piecrust folded over into the half-moon shape of a classic pasty, it is a hunter's staple.

Ingredients
    3 pounds venison, chopped
    3 pounds beef suet (do not substitute)
    3 quarts apples, finely chopped
    3 pounds seeded raisins, finely chopped
    2 pounds currants, finely chopped
    1 pound citron, cut in small pieces
    ½ C candied orange peel, chopped
    ½ C candied lemon peel, chopped
    ½ C lemon juice

¼ C orange juice
2 T salt
4 C sugar
1 C cold coffee
2 C apple cider
1 t cloves
1 t allspice
2 t cinnamon
3 C brandy
1 C sherry
1 C currant jelly (can substitute any red jelly such as blackberry, blueberry, or grape)

Mix all ingredients except brandy and sherry. Bring to a boil, reduce heat, and simmer for two hours. Remove from heat. When mixture is cool but not cold, add brandy and sherry. These two ingredients act as preservatives. If the mincemeat mixture is too hot and they are cooked off, the mincemeat will mold. Place in heavy crock, press down to remove as much air as possible, and let stand for a week. Makes 12 quarts. Will keep in a cool place, and also freezes well.

× THE OFFAL
Deer heart and liver should be eaten as fresh as possible. They can be immersed in water and frozen, but must be thawed slowly in the refrigerator, never in the microwave, and the frozen version is never as good as fresh. For those who enjoy offal, fresh deer liver is simply incomparable.

× DEER HEART

Ingredients
    1 fresh deer heart, soaked overnight in clean, very cold water, changed frequently
    1 C port

½ pound bacon, minced
1 yellow onion, minced
2-3 medium carrots, minced
2 garlic cloves, crushed
1 bay leaf
1 cup red wine
Salt and pepper, to taste

Wash and clean the heart, removing all membranes, arteries and veins. Pat dry, and slice as thinly as possible. Place slices in a medium bowl, cover with port, add salt and pepper, and marinate overnight in the refrigerator. Using a large sauté pan, cook bacon at medium heat until fat renders but the bits are not crisp. Add onion, carrots, and garlic to the fat, cooking over medium heat until onion is translucent but not browned. Turn heat to high. Lift heart slices out of port marinade, and sauté quickly until just browned. Add bay leaf, port marinade, and enough red wine to cover. Bring to a boil, then lower heat to simmer. Allow liquids to reduce. Do not overcook. Remove pan from heat and allow to rest. Remove bay leaf; add salt and pepper to taste. Serve with creamy polenta, roasted red peppers, and asparagus. Serves four to six.

× FRIED VENISON LIVER

Ingredients
1 pound venison liver, soaked in cold water
1 C flour or fine cornmeal
1 t freshly cracked black pepper
1 t salt
Three slices of thick uncured bacon, diced
One large sweet onion, sliced thinly
A pinch of red pepper flakes
½ C bacon fat or vegetable oil
1 t minced garlic

Remove membrane and arteries from the liver, and slice as thinly as possible. Pour very hot boiling water over the slices. Lift out, rinse and pat dry. In a shallow dish, mix together flour, salt, and black pepper. Dredge slices of liver in the flour, salt, and pepper mixture, and set aside (dredging can be skipped, or substitute finely ground cornmeal for a gluten-free option). Dice bacon, add sliced onions, red pepper flakes, and minced garlic, and sauté in pan until bacon is crisp and onions are translucent. Remove onion mixture from pan. Add oil to same pan and heat until fat is melted. Add coated liver slices to the fat and fry until edges are golden and crispy, about 1 minute; then flip the liver and fry the other side. Do not overcook. Remove slices and serve with sliced onions.

⤬ **THE BARBECUE RESCUE**
Because no collection of venison recipes is complete without one barbecue recipe, here it is. This one will make the toughest, gamiest chunk of venison possible to eat, if not exactly delightful. For those who enjoy hot sauces, try the Thai sauce known as sriracha, a blend of chili peppers, vinegar, garlic, and other spices. Sriracha can be mixed with mayonnaise to make a dipping sauce.

Ingredients
>   3-4 pounds of venison, cut into large chunks (irregular is fine)
>   3 celery ribs, chopped
>   1 large onion, chopped
>   1 green pepper, chopped

Barbecue sauce
>   1 C ketchup
>   1 6-oz can tomato paste
>   1 C brown sugar
>   ¼ C apple cider vinegar

3 T chili powder, more to taste
3 T lemon juice
2 T molasses
2 t salt
2 t Worcestershire sauce
1 T ground mustard

Chicken stock, as needed.
8-10 hamburger or sandwich rolls
Hot sauce

Place venison, celery, onion, and green pepper in a slow cooker. In a nonreactive bowl, place the ketchup, tomato paste, brown sugar, vinegar, chili powder, lemon juice, molasses, salt, Worcestershire sauce, and mustard. Whisk until smooth, and pour over the venison. Cover and set the cooker to Low. Cook for 9 hours or until meat is tender. Periodically check the meat to make sure that it isn't drying out; if too dry, add chicken stock.

Remove and shred the venison. Serve with buns or rolls with hot sauce on the side. Serves eight to ten.

BIBLIOGRAPHY

Primary Sources

Beeton, Isabella. *Mrs. Beeton's Manual of Household Management*. London: S. O. Beeton Publishing, 1861.

Buchanan, G. B. "Deer Hunting," in *Hunter-Trader-Trapper*, vol. 32, 1916, 25-29.

Hanbury, David. *Sport and Travel in the Northland of Canada*. London: Edward Arnold, 1904.

Hearne, Samuel. *A Journey from Prince of Wales's Fort in Hudson's Bay, to the Northern Ocean*, [1795], ed. Joseph Burr Tyrrell, Ontario: 1911.

Ortega Y Gasset, José. *Meditations on Hunting*. New York: Charles Scribner's Sons, 1972.

Secondary Sources

Bestul, Scott, and David Hurtea. *Total Deer Hunter's Manual (Field & Stream)*. N.l.: Weldon Owen, 2013.

Bittman, Mark. *How to Cook Everything*. Rev. ed. New York: Houghton Mifflin Harcourt, 2008.

Cornell Waste Management Institute, *Pathogen Analysis of NYSDOT Road-Killed Deer Carcass Compost Facilities for Task Assignment C-04-01 PIN R020.63.881 Temperature and Pathogen Final Report* (September 17, 2008). https://www.dot.ny.gov/divisions/engineering/technical-services/trans-r-and-d-repository/C-04-01%20final%20report.pdf?nd=nysdot

Davey, C. L., et al. "Carcass Electrical Stimulation to Prevent Cold Shortening in Beef," *New Zealand Journal of Agricultural Research* (Feb.-Nov. 1976): 13-18.

Festa-Bianchet, Marco, et al. "Decrease in horn size and increase in age of trophy sheep in Alberta over 37 years," *Journal of Wildlife Management* 78 no. 1 (Jan 2014): 133-41.

Gillette, F. L., and Hugo Ziemann. *The White House Cookbook*. N.l. n.p. 1887.

Gorton, Audrey Allen. *The Venison Book*. Vermont: Stephen Green Press, 1957.

Hinrichs, Uta, et al. "Data Mining Uncovers 18th century Britain's Fat Habit," *The Conversation* (April 2014).

Koller, Lawrence. *Shots at Whitetails: A Hunting Classic* [1954]. Repr. New York: Krause, 1970; 2000.

Lee, Paula, ed. *Meat, Modernity, and the Rise of the Slaughter-house*. Durham, NH: University Press of New England, 2006.

Leonard, Christopher. *The Meat Racket*. New York: Simon & Schuster, 2014.

Petersen, David. *A Hunter's Heart: Honest Essays on a Blood Sport*. New York: Henry Holt, 1996.

Pratt, J. M. 1977. "Pre-rigor high-pressure treatment effects on selected quality characteristics of beef semitendinosus muscle." MS Thesis. Oregon State University, Corvallis, OR.

Roth, Stephen M. "Why does lactic acid build up in muscles? And why does it cause soreness?" *Scientific American* (Jan. 23, 2006).

Simons, Craig. *The Devouring Dragon: How China's Rise Threatens Our Natural World*. New York: St. Martin's Press, 2013.

Vialles, Noelie. *Animal to Edible*. New York: Cambridge University Press, 1994.

INDEX